TV COVERS THE ACTION

To get the full impact of how TV covers the action, the authors follow a Washington TV bureau through a typical day, then ride with a lone mobile reporter through an action-filled night. They are there when the President talks to the press; they hear firsthand stories of combat and race riots; they speak to the news directors of the three major networks and interview outstanding correspondents and news reporters. They watch the minute-to-minute technical problems of newscasting and are impressed by the spirit of responsibility and self-criticism of those working to improve TV news. What emerges is an exciting picture of challenge and change in a vital industry that has not yet reached its tremendous potential.

Books by George N. Gordon and Irving A. Falk

ON-THE-SPOT REPORTING
Radio Records History

TV COVERS THE ACTION

YOUR CAREER IN TV AND RADIO

TV Covers the Action

by
George N. Gordon
&
Irving A. Falk

Foreword by Walter Cronkite

Illustrated with photographs

JULIAN MESSNER **NEW YORK**

Published simultaneously in the United States and Canada by
Julian Messner, a division of Simon & Schuster, Inc.,
1 West 39 Street, New York, N.Y. 10018. All rights reserved.

Dedication:

For a sister, Florence Falk,
and a brother, Eric C. Gordon

Printed in the United States of America
Library of Congress Catalog Card No. 68-25108

ACKNOWLEDGMENTS

We have only limited space to gratefully acknowledge the assistance given to us by the following people, among the many who have made this book possible: Everett Aspinwall, Gene Brandus, Irwin Chapman, Bruce Cohn, John Davenport, Petey Donaldson, John Gallagher, Dan Hackel, Robert Hemmig, Al Recht, Erdman Reck, Richard Saunders and Ed Stern of ABC Washington; Robert Fleming, Deputy Press Secretary at the White House; Len Deibert, Larry Graham, Jerry Johnson, Larry Krebs, Ted McDowell, Heywood Meeks, Ron Meninger, Herb Rosen, Morris Semiatin, Marty Swank and Foster Wiley of WMAL-TV Washington; Richard Connelly, Martin Grove, Elmer Lower and Les Schecter of ABC New York; Sig Bajak, Milton Brown, Bill Corrigan, Rex Goad, Jim Harper, George Heinemann, Jim Holton, Mac Johnson, William McAndrew, Don Meaney, Buck Prince, Russ Tornabene and Lem Tucker of NBC; Charles Collingwood, Walter Cronkite, Marshall Davidson, Rosemarie Ferrara, Charlotte Friel, Mort Goldberg, Al Goldstein, Richard Hottelet, Robert Little, Martin Pinsker, Richard Salant, Michael Silver and Mike Wallace of CBS; Ernie Angiulo, Michael Fales, George W. Headley, Jr., G. Warren Jiegler, Al Nowicki and Jerry Schur of Hofstra University; Miriam Bond, Deborah Hyson, Stephanie J. Johnson, Joanne E. Morrison and Gloria Stevenson of New York University; Grace and Frank Shane for special interests; Anna Friedman for the manuscript; and Gertrude Blumenthal for editorial advice and guidance. And many thanks to those who helped and whom space precludes our mentioning.

FOREWORD

"Television is the most powerful communications medium yet devised."

This has become a cliché because it is a simple statement of a simple truth.

Yet, for all its power and its impact, television is not a complete news medium. It lacks two essentials to so qualify: time and permanence.

Television can do *most* communication chores far better than print or unidimensional radio. Better than any other medium it can familiarize the public with the people who make the news and the places where news is made.

It achieves the ultimate through its ability to transport the chairborne viewer to the scene where news is being made. It can background the news with all the visual aids that ingenuity of man can provide — and thus capture the interest of the otherwise uncommitted.

But for all these advantages, television still can only take its place *alongside* print media as a prime source of the news.

Someday, perhaps sooner than later, the regularly scheduled news periods will be expanded, but there is a limit to that expansion. The attention span of even the most inquisitive viewer cannot be expected to stretch over the hours required to provide, in one evening, *all* the news that a good citizen requires.

Within the limited time available to it, television cannot carry specialized news of business and commerce and the public's affairs (vital statistics and the like), nor, if it could, would it provide also this material in even semi-permanent form for study and detailed examination and, possibly, future reference.

These are our handicaps and yet, so completely have

we been accepted by the public as a prime source of news (as established by qualified surveys), that we are in increasing danger of being charged with a responsibility we cannot discharge.

It would be a tragedy if either the public on the outside or some of us on the inside should be deluded into believing that, simply because we are powerful, we can do the whole job of news communication alone. Or if the public should lose confidence in television news because it failed to understand our limitations and mistook them for indolence or worse.

It is hoped, therefore, that the circulation of this book will extend beyond the journalism classrooms and that its exhaustive definition of the difficulties and the limitations of television news will reach the general public.

For a public to be well-informed, it must include in its knowledge an awareness of the limitations of its source of knowledge.

This book should help.

∗∗∗∗∗∗∗∗∗∗∗∗∗

Walter Cronkite
4/17/68
New York

CONTENTS

1

Pictures Don't Lie — Much

"I believe it because I saw it!"

How many times have you heard someone say this? Perhaps you think it is true.

Despite the fact that people have seen almost everything, from flying saucers to flying elephants, many of us believe that pictures — or, at least, photographs — cannot lie, and that we get a more realistic idea of the world around us from pictures than from words. Newspapers like the great photographic tabloids here and in England have gathered enormous circulations because of their pictorial coverage of the news. Millions of copies of picture magazines like *Life* are sold weekly all around the world.

Just a century ago, however, a photograph had not yet been printed in a single American newspaper! Woodcuts and other types of drawings — including steel fashion plates — were familiar by this time in printed documents. The invention of the zincograph, by which pictures were etched on metal by means of acid, was introduced to the

United States in 1870, and shortly thereafter newspapers began printing hand-copied photographs which were traced by artists directly onto wood or metal printing blocks by means of either an etching tool or acid.

As late as 1891, more than 1,000 artists were professionally involved in tracing pictures for publication in our newspapers and magazines. The process of photoengraving, which is employed for printing many types of photographs today, was invented by Frederic E. Ives, head of the photographic laboratory at Cornell University as early as 1878. But the process was not perfected until later, and it was not until 1897 that Ives's halftone reproductions were printed in the *New York Tribune*, a historic event which literally changed the face of newspapers all over the world during the following decade. After the invention of photoengraving, not only photographs, but drawings and paintings and almost any kind of art work could be accurately and simply reproduced by the photoengraving processes, both with black and with various-colored inks, depending on how many times paper was run through the process to achieve combinations of colors.

Photojournalism was naturally dependent upon the invention, progress and perfection (which is still going on) of photography. Many people believe, the authors among them, that the invention of the photograph — generally credited to the Frenchmen Louis Daguerre and Joseph Nicéphore Niepce, an Englishman, Henry Fox Talbot, and a number of their fellow countrymen who were experimenting with light-sensitive materials between 1822 and 1840 — was one of the most important developments of the nineteenth century. This invention alone and its progress from the crude, hardly visible metal prints made in the 1820s and 1830s to the modern color Polaroid film of today is itself a long and exciting story which not only affected journalism and all forms of printing, but also produced deep and lasting effects on the arts and sciences of our day.

At the same time that ingenious tinkerers were developing ways to reproduce photographs quickly and cheaply on printing presses, another invention was incubating—a little gadget with names like the Zoëtrope, Stroboscope, Proximoscope, Kinetoscope and Zoöproxinascope. Who invented the motion pictures? No one can answer this question for certain, largely because the cinema depends on so many devices and inventions, involved in the photographing of a sequence of pictures on one hand and instruments for displaying them on the other. Some of the people who are—correctly—credited with the development of the motion pictures are the Lumière brothers and Dr. E. J. Marey in France, William Friese-Greene in England and Thomas Edison and his assistant William Dickson in America.

The claim of most of the "inventors," however, is frequently challenged by the assertion that all each did was perfect a process of photography and exhibition either designed or developed by someone else. This is probably the truth, because the development of the motion picture from the middle 1800s through the introduction of sound film in the 1920s up until the present moment has been a collaborative process, not the result of any one stroke of genius. It has been reflective more of the solution of problems by *technology* than of the application of *scientific thinking* to theory.

At first, it was the still cameraman who followed the men who followed the news. In 1855, Roger Fenton, an English photographer, traveled with British troops to the famous battle of Balaklava in the Crimea and returned with hundreds of pictures of the men, and their equipment, who participated in the ill-fated "charge of the light brigade." During the next decade an American named Mathew Brady, assisted by Alexander Gardner and Timothy O'Sullivan (both of whom were first-rate photographers in their own right, credit for whose work has frequently gone to Brady), made the first incisive, relatively complete record in photographs of the American Civil War from the perspective of the Northern Army. Brady had at his command twenty-two teams—or crews, as we would call them today—each of which took pictures of the conflict. They had to develop their highly unstable photographic plates in tents and other improvised darkrooms uncomfortably close to the front lines of battle.

"Brady's photographs" (many of them taken and developed by his assistants) constitute as fine a pictorial record as exists today of a segment of history. They are all the more remarkable when you consider the primitive equipment with which he and his crews had to work, the time exposures necessary and other limitations of the medium. If, however, we have a notion of how the Civil War in fact looked to the men who fought it—the sweating, bearded and moustached long-haired men in cumbersome blue uniforms carrying their crude rifles and filling their tortuously heavy cannons with explosives and (to us) laughable lead cannon balls, the dead lying on the battlefields at sunset or the faces of the generals and their staff plotting the course of warfare in their crude command tents—it is because Mathew Brady's photographs have so eloquently preserved this historic episode for us. In many ways, no photographer since Brady has introduced such a style of coverage and so personal an editorial viewpoint of an event. This is largely because Brady had to work within the crude limitations of the medium of his day and concentrate on aspects of the conflict which it was possible for the camera to record faithfully.

With the invention of the halftone and the work of Brady to inspire them, a new breed of photojournalists was developed in the last part of the nineteenth century. Newspapers like the New York *Graphic* made photographs their main stock in trade, and in other imitative papers similar to it—particularly the *New York Daily News* some years later—many journalists discovered that few news stories existed which could not be complemented by a photograph of some kind to add spice and interest to their coverage.

Documentary photographers like Jacob A. Riis and Lewis W. Hine took their cameras with them to draw a portrait of a nation—not the portrait in the lyrics of "America the Beautiful," but pictures of the urban poor, the immigrants whose labor was exploited in our factories, children at work in sweat shops and Negroes who had been freed from slavery for a more horrible kind of exploitation at the hands of Southern industrialists and farmers. Their photographs during the first decade of this century (and Hine's work up until 1932) made of the art of photography an instrument freed from the studio sittings and the cumbersome developing apparatus of men like Mathew Brady. The stories that Riis and Hine wanted to tell were located in the world beyond the usual paths photographers trod, and they traveled to them, cameras in hand. Their object was to reveal effectively, and frequently shockingly, the squalor in which millions of Americans lived in order to awaken the public to the social evils which our society was tolerating and about which much had to be done to correct them.

Their pictures were still pictures, but, viewed in sequence, they frequently constituted a narrative essay which made a specific point. Other, less serious photographers attempted the same sort of coverage by interviewing celebrities, covering society functions and sporting events and whatever spot news an individual photographer was lucky enough to run into—or to contrive or fake, which was frequently the case. Such photo-stories were the fore-runners of the modern photographic essay of the type you'll find in *Life* magazine or in a tabloid newspaper: a sequence of pictures of the rescue of an attempted suicide or a fire or some other event of pictorial interest.

The development of the newsreel, or the motion picture equivalent of this narrative kind of photographic coverage, dates back to about the same period as the invention of the photo-essay itself. Films that may be called "newsreels" have been found among the oldest cans of film in library archives, undoubtedly because it was recognized early that the cinema offered enormous possibilities for keeping the record of history even more accurately and dramatically than still photographs. In the early days of the movies, when short films were displayed in inexpensive theaters called "Nickelodeons" (because the charge for admission was five cents), producers like J. Stuart Blackton and Albert Smith of the Vitograph Corporation competed with "theatrical" or re-enacted films (consisting of scenes from contemporary plays) by showing movie newsreels of the Boer and Spanish American wars. According to the record, movie makers of their stripe were not adverse, frequently, to faking an "on-the-spot" newsreel with models.

Newsreels were never as successful as theatrical films, however, and remain up to the present day adjuncts or program fillers for theatrical fiction films. Almost from their earliest days, audiences preferred to see movie stars in their dream-dramas rather than to be faced with reality. Thanks to enterprising and dedicated film pioneers like the Lumière brothers, the Pathé brothers and Leon Gaumont in France and Edison in America, we have today remark-ably complete records of life in Paris and New York during the end of the last century and the beginning of this one and films of such remote events as the inauguration of President McKinley in 1896 here in the U.S.A.

As the twentieth century grew older, many cinema producers recognized that audiences enjoyed newsreels and came to expect them as part of their moviegoing experience. While the great fortunes—and fame—went to the producers and stars of feature films, the preparation of a weekly or semiweekly newsreel was a moderately lucrative business that was—as opposed to much film production—relatively secure and stable. At first, most of the newsreel production firms were independently owned, but by the 1920s (a period during which the motion pictures became a major American industry) most of them had been absorbed by the big film companies, which distributed newsreels regularly to exhibitions along with their output of feature films.

One important question about these early newsreels—and the ones that followed them up until the 1950s—was: What is news? The answer was painfully simple: news was what the audience was interested in! And so a format of newsreel coverage was evolved which covered, in rapid succession (and eventually with a narrative sound track) a smorgasbord of man-made disasters like wars and fires, natural catastrophes like hurricanes, earthquakes and landslides, the latest fashions in women's wear, an inevitable sequence about animals in a zoo, sporting events from skiing to chess, interviews with politicians and foreign royalty visiting the U.S.A., pre-election coverage (which gave the audience a chance to applaud their favorite candidate) and a segment featuring the Hollywood preview of the "latest and greatest" movie from Hollywood, invariably produced by the same company which made the newsreel. The whole enterprise rarely ran for more than ten minutes, but it represented, for most of the people in the audience, the only opportunity they had to view at close hand the men and events that had made the headlines of their daily papers during the preceding weeks. That they were also filled with fun, games and nonsense was simply evidence of what the film makers knew well: the bulk of the audience went to the movies for laughs and "kicks" and was not interested in serious news.

Nor was the audience particularly interested in the daring photographers who had risked their lives during World War I (and later World War II), traveled to forest fires, covered the far-off wars, like the invasion of Manchuria in the early 1930s or the Spanish Civil War later in the decade, and carried their cameras into primitive aircraft, behind a motorboat on water skis or on a suicidal bobsled run to provide interesting footage for the Saturday-night gangs who flocked by millions into local movie theaters.

Looking back on some of these films, it is difficult to understand why audiences were so indifferent to them, except that, until World War II shook us to our senses, the great mass of Americans were apathetic and indifferent to most matters beyond their pleasures. They certainly did not want to be forced to consume a dose of harsh reality in a movie theater! They had paid their hard cash for Hollywood's dream world, and dreams were what they wanted in return from the shadows on the screen.

True, occasional film makers were successful (at least, artistically) with news features of a kind they called "documentary films" — a type of motion picture which, to date, in both theatrical movies and on TV has not recaptured the promise or excellence it showed in its earliest days. This was a period during the past generation when men like John Grierson in England and Robert Flaherty in America were telling their cinematic stories about common men around the world from the Arctic to the factories of Great Britain by means of well-photographed and well-edited documentary films. Setting out to recapture some facet of real life and telling it in brilliant cinematic terms, these two pioneers had their followers and imitators, who continue to this day the laudable attempt to create a type of nonfiction, well-edited filmic commentary, lasting more than a few minutes, on a serious issue of some sort. Their names are now part of cinematic history: Louis de Rochemont, creator of "The March of Time" films, Basil Wright, Pare Lorentz and — ironically, probably the greatest of them all — Leni Riefenstahl, whose documentaries extolled the glories of Nazi Germany and Adolph Hitler.

Numerous film makers, most of them involved also with fiction films, tried their hands at documentary, particularly when World War II created a demand for their services. Carol Reed, Garson Kanin, Frank Capra and John Huston were among them, and their films about the war, produced both for the military men who were going off to fight and for the civilian audiences back home, have become classics.

Great as their contributions to film art have been — and fascinating as their work remains to this day — there is little doubt that the art of the film documentary has never lived up to the high aspirations or remarkable models that its originators set for it decades ago. Flaherty's *Nanook of the North* was never duplicated in quality, even by its own producer-director. Neither have more recent attempts to produce similar films been more than moderately successful. Some, like those produced by the National Film Board of Canada (for example, *City of Gold* and *Lonely Boy*), have been of passing interest, as have Lionel Rogosin's works (particularly his early film *On the Bowery*), but they kept interest in the documentary film alive. At both the New York World's Fair of 1965 – 66 and Canada's

Expo '67, some interesting industrial and political documentaries were displayed, but films shown in the pseudo-environment of a World's Fair almost invariably seem better than they really are.

Without question, the documentary film (and documentary TV show) has, at its best, lagged pitifully behind the *best* work done by producers, writers and directors of both serious and comic fiction films. With the exception, perhaps, of the originators of the documentary and the ex-Nazi, Miss Riefenstahl, they—for the most part—hardly justify a cinematic second place to the outstanding feature films. Even the best are dated quickly, as the rush of events turn them obsolete. Most of them either smash their editorial fist so hard into the viewers' eyes or arrive so gently, subtlely or cutely at their social, political or religious "point" that they fail to provide the complete and meaningful experience which even a good cinematic farce-comedy can generate.

Film makers appear to be competent to re-create "unreality" with amazing success, considering the number of excellent fiction films made the world over—including Hollywood U.S.A. They seem to have much more trouble re-creating "reality" itself, either by photographing denizens of their own settings "reliving" their daily lives or by manufacturing in a cutting room a nonfiction film from clips of old newsreel films combined with the 20-20 vision of perfect hindsight, in the form of a pretentious narration read by an actor with a cultivated baritone.

The reason is, probably, that reality is extremely hard to re-create, even if you use "authentic" actors and settings as documentary film makers do. Film and TV cameras are almost impossible to "fool." The eye of the camera takes pictures of things as they are; the sound track records the noises of life as they exist in life. When, therefore, directors blatantly tell an audience that what they are showing them is not real life (which they do implicitly in the case of every fiction film made) the unreality of what the camera sees and what the sound track says is acceptable to you and me. We are being fooled, but it is fun to be fooled—as anyone who has seen a good magician knows!

When, on the other hand, we are asked to believe that a camera is showing us the world the way it is but we are shown that world the way a director or producer wants us to see it, we are victims of a fraud seriously intended, and therefore we are not fooled, and it is not fun! This is the central problem of the documentary film: it pretends to a reality it *cannot* achieve because, by its nature, it must distort reality for "artistic" reasons—that is, to make the point (or carry the propaganda) which the producer had in mind.

Documentary film and its growth have been extremely important—perhaps vital—in the development of another kind of pictorial coverage by motion pictures and TV: on-the-spot live, filmed or taped coverage of news of all kinds *as it happens.* In coverage of this kind *nothing* is re-created. The camera is covering the action, and not the cameraman, the director or a member of the audience (in live broadcasts) is ever entirely certain how the event will end. Nobody is fooled, and every second is frequently as exciting as the most skillfully told drama that professional directors, writers and actors have ever produced!

2

The Rise of Radio

The great period of radio broadcasting lasted twenty years and stretched, roughly, from 1928 to 1948.

By the time it was well over, technologists, oddly, had managed to perfect the instrument which solved the main difficulties in on-the-spot broadcasting. The gadget was the electronic transistor, which permitted the miniaturization of both broadcasting and reception equipment beyond the wildest dreams of the intrepid broadcasters who, in the early days, carried carloads of cumbersome equipment to a stadium or meeting hall to cover action as it happened for their listeners.

The transistors arrived just in time to witness the diminution of national radio network broadcasting in the United States and see it shrink from a major news medium to a number of local enterprises. Our people own more radio sets today than ever in history: *at least* one for every man, woman and child in our population. Tape recorders and broadcasting equipment a child can use — and carry — flood the market. It is cheap and it works! Ironically, it came along too late and missed the deadline, the cut-off point of the wonderful and exciting era of sound broadcasting.

The story of how radio recorded history from the days immediately after World War I until the introduction of coast-to-coast TV has been told from different viewpoints by many witnesses. We have written a book about it our-selves — *On-the-Spot Reporting: Radio Records History.* It will be told many times and in many ways again, be-cause it was an incredible time of experimentation and excitement, of novelty and failure and of innovation and success.

In a nutshell, the radio spot news medium was born and developed in the United States along with the most incred-ibly wealthy and commercial system of broadcasting in the entire world, the only one which was turned over almost entirely to private managers and businessmen to operate for their own profit.

Profit they did! From the day in August in 1922 when a real-estate man read the first commercial over station WEAF in New York City to the present moment, radio has by and large been a financial gold mine for the men who sell "time" to local and national sponsors. Broadcast-ers' objectives, therefore, quickly became that of amassing the largest audience possible to "deliver" reliably to poten-tial advertisers. Early in the game, they discovered some-thing that every high school student in America knows today: that people would rather laugh and joke than deal with genuine problems, that they prefer fantasy to reality and that they would rather relax than be challenged to think.

To amass other large audiences, the national networks (two of which are following their well-worn tracks of radio days into TV-land) NBC, CBS and subsequently MBS flooded the airwaves with programs that their managers were convinced were "what the people wanted." And the people had no choice—this was what they got.

What is remarkable is that, along with this carnival of commercialism, the radio industry, shoulder to shoulder with its advertisers and its agencies, developed means and methods for broadcasting on-the-spot news that not only could and did compete with the comics and hucksters but actually made history. Exactly why and how it happened, we do not know. Perhaps the radio audience was a bit more sophisticated than the "best brains in broadcasting" thought they were. Perhaps certain radio industry leaders like William Paley and David Sarnoff not only *said* that radio had an obligation to inform as well as entertain but actually meant it. Most serious students of broadcasting were—and are—skeptical of the quoted remarks of leaders of an industry which courted fantastic yearly profits as avidly as radio broadcasters did. Nevertheless, the miracle occurred.

The fact remains that serious live coverage of news events was far less profitable than standard, sponsored, commercial network broadcasts—with the significant exception of sporting events. The fact also remains that, from the early 1920s onwards, the magnificent men with their wireless machines broadcast the news from everywhere: from miles high in stratosphere balloons to submarine bathyspheres, from the floor of political convention halls to the battlefields of World War II. Some broadcasters, like Ted Husing and Graham McNamee, talked, shouted, yelled and laughed themselves into sickbeds covering political conventions and events of state. Some, like Norman Brokenshire and Boake Carter, were driven by the insanities of their labors and their peculiar natures to personal tragedy and recovery and back to tragedy. Some, like

Maurice Hindus and William Shirer, went on to notable careers in fields outside radio broadcasting. Some, like Tom Traynor, were killed in the war.

Others rose to a stature unique in the history of news reporting. Is it unfitting to compare the broadcasts of Edward R. Murrow during the London *blitzkreig* of 1941 with the photographs of Mathew Brady depicting the American Civil War? We think not. Both men were reporters, using their unique talents in relatively new media to bring vivid pictures of warfare to a public that would otherwise have remained ignorant of the *quality* of the era in which they were living. Both men directed teams of other reporters who learned their craft from inventive and talented innovators; and both men preserved more than a surface facade of humility as their eyes beheld the terror and impact of the world around them which they attempted to report as accurately and meaningfully as possible.

The structure of remote on-the-spot news coverage evolved out of the trials and errors of the radio broadcasters who manned the news microphones of the networks during the great commercial age of radio broadcasting. No *one* man was responsible for the development or perfection of techniques allied to this kind of coverage. Trials were many and errors were frequent.

When a great remote on-the-spot broadcast did occur—like James Bowen's description of the scuttling of the German battleship *Graf Spee* in Montevideo harbor on December 14, 1939—it frequently happened more or less by accident. A reporter with sufficient equipment, sometimes no more than a telephone connection, was at the right place at the right time, and the message he delivered made history. This was what happened to a young journalist by the name of Eric Sevareid who found himself the last American capable of broadcasting to the United States as the Germans were marching into the city of Paris, France, on June 9, 1940. His first and last report from that conquered area not only became a broadcasting legend, but was also to become one of the many fine examples of how broadcasters were willing to risk their personal safety and security to bring to the American audience an accurate, immediate description of news as it was happening. Severeid's name is just one of many whose voices the American public heard from the battlefronts, newsfronts and disaster areas of the world during the great years of radio broadcasting.

They were voices we heard all too infrequently. How fortunate that so many of us today remember the medium of radio by its finest moments! The history we write may be highly selective, but so is the history of most other institutions: the press, medicine, education, architecture or aviation.

Not all radio history was made directly in front of the microphone. Managers and executives were also responsible for the growth of on-the-spot radio broadcasting in equal measure with the reporters themselves. Most of these innovators have been lost in the shuffle of history, but their basic motive was a response to crisis that, oddly enough, had begun in the front offices of newspaper wire services and in the editorial rooms of daily newspapers across the nation.

By the time the major networks were organized, it had become sufficiently clear to all concerned that radio broadcasting was a potentially powerful information medium. The publishers of American newspapers became frightened. Would the public stop—or cut down on—reading of papers? They felt there was little sense in taking a chance and accordingly cut off the legitimate supply of news via the teletype wire services to radio broadcasters, services upon which the newspapers themselves were vitally dependent. A network, a station, was literally barred from membership in the Associated Press, United Press or International News Services, among others.

The managers of the broadcasting outlets had a choice. They were obviously involved in a war with the press, a war which had, by the 1930s, reached such bitter dimensions that newspapers frequently refused to publish the daily list of entertainment programs (to say nothing of news broadcasts) presented on local radio stations. Broadcasters, had they wished, could have accepted defeat and – at first glance, to their own advantage – have gone out of the news business entirely, concentrating on the more highly profitable production of comedy shows, soap operas, musical programs and other forms of pure entertainment.

They chose to stand and fight the journalist probably for three reasons. First, since the first broadcasts in the early 1920s by Pittsburgh's pioneer station KDKA, radio innovators had clearly demonstrated that they could offer news coverage of a type that printed newspapers could not. Radio was a faster medium than print; it could spread a news story to communities or across the nation in seconds while newspapers took hours. It could also bring the listener to the place where news was happening; its on-the-spot broadcasts were a type of coverage impossible for newspapers – even picture newspapers – to duplicate. Second, the public had demonstrated that it wanted news broadcasts. Early news analysts like Lowell Thomas became figures of renown overnight, and it was obvious that millions of listeners were literally glued to their radio sets at political convention time, for major prizefights and baseball games and to listen to the speeches of statesmen and visiting foreign leaders as well as national heroes.

Third, the Communications Act of 1934, a law of Congress setting up a commission for the control of broadcasting in the United States, clearly stated that all commercial broadcasters were bound by legislation to act in "the public interest, convenience and necessity." How could they accomplish this directive and ignore the news of the day in their broadcasting?

Fight they did—in a number of ways. CBS set up what remains to this day probably both the largest and the best news gathering agency for broadcasting in the country. The late Paul White was given the money and authority to hire reporters all over the world to replace the missing news service tickertapes in the CBS newsrooms in New York. Such an agency was difficult to organize, and, shortly befor his death, Ed Murrow recalled that each CBS news broadcast in the middle thirties ended with the statement: "For details, see your daily newspaper," a sly admission that CBS daily coverage was far from adequate. But by the time World War II began, CBS had a news staff comparable to that of the journalists' wire service which continues to the present on TV and radio.

Abe Schecter, director of news for NBC in those days, did not have the resources at his command that White had at CBS. But he had some fine newsmen like Lowell Thomas, George Hicks and others, and he had contacts around the world who fed his bureau enough daily news to compete effectively with CBS. Sometimes the two major networks, both suffering the exclusion from conventional news sources, would divide the wealth by helping each other cover notable news events. Other networks, including the Mutual chain, were highly dependent on "stringers," part-time correspondents around the nation and the world who would be activated for news broadcasting as stories "broke" in their respective areas.

Radio was not providing serious competition for the newspapers (in fact, they were soon to learn that both media could prosper side by side), but it was clearly demonstrating its effectiveness and independence from the major sources of news open to the working press. Broadcasters, in fact, had even begun operating their own news service, Trans-Radio Press, which serviced radio broadcasters almost entirely.

By the time World War II had begun in Europe, the major wire services had capitulated. As the result of pressures from many directions (including the Federal Government, which was concerned about monopoly practices), radio stations were finally permitted membership in press associations. Most newspaper publishers also discovered that printed logs of daily radio programs increased rather than cut down on their daily circulations. Radio newscasters began to be treated by newspapermen as journalists; they were free now to join their organizations, carry bona fide press cards, and consider themselves "reporters," not just "radio personalities."

The broadcasters, however, were in no mood to give up the unique news-gathering services they had developed in the years that they had been excluded from the wire services by the journalists. What they have been forced to do, of course, was develop new and effective ways to gather and report news, and they were not inclined to unlearn the insights they had gained, methods they had evolved and highly skilled staffs of radio reporters they had trained. A great war was on the horizon, and the combined talents of all the broadcasters in America, as well as newspaper journalists and wire service personnel, would be needed to cover the far-flung action that was to engulf nearly the entire globe in its fire and brimstone for the next five years.

How radio broadcasters reported to the American public

World War II and its incredible aftermath will not be treated in this book. As a footnote to history, let us merely add here that the first remote on-the-spot *telecasts* were made by the National Broadcasting Company on December 12, 1937, and the first regular telecasting in America began two years later, in 1939, from station W2XBS, New York. Nothing new was heard or seen from this infant medium for quite a few years after that. But when baby began crying, he received plenty of attention!

3

The People Are Watching

Our system of television broadcasting, with its more than 700 stations—over 150 of which are educational, noncommercial operations—is undoubtedly the richest in the world. Nothing quite like our three major networks and their system of affiliated station outlets exists anywhere else. Many TV services, even those run by government agencies, broadcast advertising; some of them are even more totally immersed in commercialism than are many American stations. In some other countries, program services are paid for by taxes levied against set owners. If you look hard enough, you will find nations where armies, the police force and even churches run major TV operations.

One generalization can easily be made about TV around the world—the non-Communist world, at least: the lion's share of what appears on the screens of TV sets in other nations is material of American origin. In other words, it is the same programming that you and I saw last year—or last season—with a sound track dubbed in a foreign tongue if necessary. That is, it is the same unless local laws limit the amount of American film and tape which may be used per day, which is the case in those nations which are attempting to stimulate local production — or discourage what they usually call "Americanization."

Suffice it to say that during the period of TV's greatest growth in the United States (roughly, from 1947 to 1957), nothing — not even the invention of radio broadcasting — like the TV boom had ever happened before! No device — not Henry Ford's Model T, or the motion picture, or the Wright brothers' airplane — infiltrated as quickly, completely and deeply into our way of life and our habits of thought and behavior as TV. Note well that TV also infiltrated into our bulging pocketbooks; its rise accompanied the greatest period of growth and prosperity through which our nation had ever lived. People bought TV sets because they loved the programs. Advertisers literally fought one another for TV time, because people were watching, convinced (probably correctly) that those of us who watched their commercials would buy their products in quantity. The more their sales charts rose, the greater their prosperity — and the prosperity of their workers, shopkeepers and stockholders — seemed to become. Result: more TV sets sold.

When color TV came, it looked as if the few skeptics left might be right and the bubble might burst! Color TV, they said, was too expensive for advertisers, and the networks (particularly NBC, whose parent company RCA had developed color TV) had to underwrite the added cost of color production. But the high prices of color TV sets started to fall, and more and more people naturally began to purchase color sets — at present writing about 17 percent of the total audience in America. As the other networks initiated tinted programming, it became highly likely that advertisers would be more than willing to take advantage of the added impact of color TV in producing their messages and paying for production. The economic miracle of TV still appeared an endless spiral.

When TV was young, it had two heritages on which to call when it came to news coverage. In the first place, TV was developed by people who had, mostly, been radio broadcasters. The techniques and traditions mentioned in the previous chapters were in their bloodstreams, and they unquestionably intended that TV news develop into the same kind of public service that radio broadcasting had been at its best. They were highly dubious about the new baby: the bulky TV cameras, the hot, bright lights necessary to obtain a decent picture and the merciless TV picture tube, which transmitted every facial flaw, every nervous flutter of a hand or the shifting eyes of a reporter reading a script, presented them with hosts of problems. Hardened reporters melted before the stare of the camera's lens and yearned for the days of their portable microphones and quiet sound studios.

In the second place, TV was obviously a visual medium, and, if current events were to be broadcast on this new device, people were going to want to look at them —or watch something—besides a newsman talking into a microphone. The tradition of photojournalism—going back to Brady and before—implied strongly that *the reporter himself must not intrude into the picture he shows his public*. The newsreels of the era of sound film (after 1927) displayed, at most, a few seconds of a narrator's face in each news segment. Ed Thorgersen, Lew Lehr, Adelaide Hawley and the other newsreel narrators (many of whom doubled as radio actors and announcers) were usually heard and not seen; their voices, sound effects and appropriate music covered the edited film of a news story.

Could TV straddle the arts of radio and newsreels? Did its broadcasters want to? Was it technically possible?

The first answer TV broadcasters gave to these problems was a tentative "yes and no." In the early days of TV, newscasters like John Cameron Swayze, Douglas Edwards and Drew Pearson—as well as familiar radio figures like Robert Trout and George Hicks—attempted to deliver "illustrated lectures" concerning the news of the day, using as many "audiovisual aids" as they could get into a TV studio. Their programs were replete with so many graphs, charts, maps, photographs (projected behind, above and below them), props, drawings and other paraphernalia that their newscasts frequently looked like junk shops.

An attempt was also made to provide as much filmed material as possible to get the camera away from the studio and onto the focal action of a news story. But where to find newsfilm? Since the TV broadcasters themselves were not equipped to shoot and develop their own movies, they were forced to buy it from established newsreel firms. Their methods of preparing one or two reels of film were far too slow and antiquated for a rapid fire medium like TV, which gobbled up news as quickly as it was made and hungered for newsclips minutes after (or during) the march of events.

One answer was the formation of relatively small—but fast and flexible—news firms like Telenews, whose main asset was speed. Providing a written script instead of a sound-on-film narration, for TV stations, these newsreel firms would ship their hastily edited films and scripts to TV stations before daily deadlines. The movie clips would give the newscasters something to narrate which was more dramatic and to the point than a map or photograph.

Another solution was the use of remote TV relays,

either by means of coaxial cable or by microwaves (beams). Where this was possible, it worked wonderfully. Coaxial connections to the United Nations building from Rockefeller Center in New York operated magnificently, so did microwave relays from baseball parks in the suburbs to TV antenna towers on top of a high building in the center of a city. But the TV signal is a difficult impulse to transmit successfully, far more resistant to long-range broadcasting than AM radio waves. The cables that carried TV signals in the early days were more costly and complex than the telephone lines which radio broadcasters so frequently used. Worse, the microwave relay beam, which carried remote TV broadcasts, traveled only in *straight lines* — like a beam of light — and thereby could be sent only to a reception point as far as the horizon, at which point it had to be re-energized and retransmitted. Radio short waves, on the other hand, followed the contours of the earth far beyond the horizon and were easy to transmit over great distances.   1457951

Problems of transmission still bother TV engineers to this day. The use of space satellites, of course, to deflect TV signals headed out into space back to earth (thereby allowing them to travel far beyond the horizon) is one workable solution. Satellites, however, must be located in exactly the right position for effective transmission, and some engineers claim that at present they do not appear to be living up to their previously expected technical potential.

Coaxial cable is still expensive, but many new uses have been found for it (including the transmission of vast amounts of computer data, telephone calls and other electronic impulses) in addition to carrying TV broadcasts, and, accordingly, millions of miles of it have been sunk beneath city streets, on plains and prairies and under bodies of water around the world. A virtual network of microwave relay stations has also been constructed, not only in the U.S.A. but abroad, to transmit TV signals from one horizon to the next over great distances. The original problem that faced TV newscasters in the infant days of TV, how to cover the news as rapidly and as fully as possible in moving images, still remains to nettle telecasters the world over, but many of its original thorns, at least, have been removed.

Wherever TV went and however it got there—by film or live coverage, by cable or through the ether—it has molded for itself a unique and effective form of news coverage. To radio broadcasting, it added pictures, mostly in motion, which vivified what had previously merely been described. To newsreels, it added the dimensions of accessibility and speed, bringing the sounds and sights of far-off events directly into our homes either as they were happening or shortly thereafter, far more conveniently, and usually more suspensefully, than the old motion picture theater newsreel.

Sports are an excellent example. Radio broadcasting was fine for contests of almost ritual sameness: baseball, football and horse racing, for instance. Prizefights are broadcast satisfactorily on radio, but they usually strain the descriptive powers of the announcer telling about them. And if you see a film of the fight you heard, you often wonder whether the sportscaster was looking at the same event you saw.

Newsreels were fine for recapping the most important action in a sporting event: the final putt at a golf tournament that clinched the winner's score, the swan dive that won the swimming meet or the line drive over the end zone that won the ball game for dear old Yale. Sometimes an entire prizefight—particularly Joe Louis' heavyweight matches in the 1930s — was shown at local movie houses the day after the event when excitement ran high. Fortunately, Louis' fights tended to be short, but many of the movie palaces showed the long ones too, round after round for fifteen rounds, although everyone in the audience naturally knew who the winner of the bout was going to be.

Now television is able to cover the spontaneous excitement of all sorts of sports *as they are happening*. Some events, like professional wrestling, even went through a period when matches were rehearsed to make them more "telegenic. Every wrestling match featured a "hero and villain." It was terrible sportsmanship and worse sport, but to an unsophisticated video audience, it was exciting TV. It has, mercifully, passed from the scene.

Legitimate professional boxing profited immeasurably from TV coverage. Unfortunately, the TV era saw a diminution in the caliber of heavyweight champions, from fighters of the professional skill of Rocky Marciano and Joe Walcott to "champions" like Sonny Liston and Ingemar Johansson. Baseball and football looked fine on the home screen, particularly the latter after the introduction of color, and golf tournaments took on a new suspense as the cameras followed the action while announcers — frequently ex-pros themselves — kept their hushed comments to a minimum. The coverage of horse racing by TV cameras was not appreciably more exciting than radio rundowns by veterans like Clem McCarthy had been, but much of the glamour and color of events, like the yearly Kentucky Derby, lent themselves to coverage by TV and stimulated interesting interviews between broadcasters, racing folk and other celebrities.

Inevitably TV developed its own kinds of athletic events it could cover best. At first — in the 1950s — the roller derby was raised to the level of a nationally popular spectator sport. Many viewers never succeeded in figuring out exactly what a roller derby was, but it involved tough-looking females on roller skates spinning around in circles hitting and bumping into each other and somehow scoring points. Doubtless, also, bowling was given a tremendous boost as a popular pastime because of extensive coverage given various tournaments on TV. Neither newsreels nor radio broadcasters had given much attention to sports like these, and their success — particularly the continued popularity of the latter — was directly related to the fact that the TV cameras were capable of capturing their suspense and the skill and cool nerve of the contestants better than other media and offered the viewer the "front row" seat he could not have had in an auditorium or bowling alley.

Most of the first, notable on-the-spot TV news coverage was broadcast live; neither film nor tape recording was as yet practical, and part of the key to the acceptance of the new medium depended on the feeling of spontaneity the public experienced while watching live TV. To many, it seems odd that the vast audience today appears to display this identical reaction to most TV programs which are usually on tape or film. There is nothing unexpected about this reaction. Habituation to TV as a "live" medium — as well as improvements and refinements in the quality of film and tape production — are the inevitable results of years of experience with the impact of crucial live programs — like election night and convention coverage — and the emphasis that TV producers put on the illusions of *immediacy* and *newness*. The name of Ed Murrow's old TV program "See It Now" sums up the general tone and stance of most TV broadcasting, especially news and documentary programs.

We were in New York City, for instance, in 1951 when a Congressional Committee headed by Senator Estes Kefauver investigated organized crime in the United States under the surveillance of the major networks' TV cameras. It is no exaggeration to say that New York, at least, was paralyzed by the telecasts! Crowds gathered on the streets, in restaurants and bars to watch the bizarre inquiry which featured the Senator, arch-gangster Frank Costello (who only permitted his hands to be televised because "da lights hoit me eyes!"), a gun moll named Virginia Hill (who looked as if she had been sent to the hearings from a casting agency), and ex-Mayor O'Dwyer of New York (who was denied permission to return to his city for a half-dozen years after the broadcasts, lest he be slapped with a summons to account for his behavior).

One received the impression that everyone — from professors to housewives — was talking about the grimy cast of thugs who faced a team of moralistic, irate Senators and a fiery young attorney named Rudy Halley, who later ran for mayor of New York and died shortly after he lost the election.

Television was unmistakably a part of life. The medium now proved beyond a shadow of a doubt that it could cover immediate action and that it was capable of penetrating deeply into human character with an immediacy and sense of excitement that neither radio nor film might hope to approach!

In 1953, TV itself made news of another kind when films of the Coronation of Queen Elizabeth II of England were flown across the Atlantic, developed and dried in the airplane which carried them, and subsequently telecast that evening over American networks. Here was live coverage of the event — almost! Radio broadcasters had described the Coronation some hours earlier, but, by evening, the radiance of the new British Queen and the majesty and ceremony of the centuries-old coronation rite were on view on TV for all of America to see.

Then, by 1954, another Senator became a familiar figure on our TV screens. His name was Joseph McCarthy, he hailed from Wisconsin, and there is little doubt today that he was propelled to a near insane fury in a sincere attempt to hunt down subversives, particularly Communists, serving (he believed) the United States Government in its civilian agencies and armed forces. McCarthy cared little for common decencies of law and order and cared even less for common sense. In his hell-bent "investigations" he damaged or ruined the reputations of many innocent people through his abuse of their democratic rights.

The people, in the end, caused the downfall of the foxy Senator from Wisconsin. They had seen one devastating portrait of him on Ed Murrow's "See It Now" TV program, but, in 1954, the Department of the Army brought charges against McCarthy resulting from his irresponsible accusations that high brass officers in the armed forces were coddling radicals. In front of the nation's TV cameras, Senator McCarthy attempted to turn the tables on the Army and prove his case. The failure and defeat brought only good news to the American public.

A Boston lawyer named Joseph Welch, various other Senators, and the Secretary of the Army demonstrated to the American people, by means of TV, exactly what kind of an unscrupulous man McCarthy was—how he would lie and pervert the truth to gain a tactical advantage, and how he used the sharp instrument of freedom of speech to silence his opponents.

As a direct result of the televised hearings, and in response to the national public outrage caused by the TV hearings, McCarthy himself was investigated by a Committee of the Senate. He was officially censured and condemned for his irresponsible behavior by his colleagues.

On the date of his censure, December 2, 1954, the

American public watched the bleary-eyed Joseph McCarthy peer at a TV camera and attempt to laugh off his punishment. "It was hardly a vote of confidence!" he chuckled into a microphone. His political career, of course, was finished, and also, ironically, so was his life. Senator Joseph McCarthy died on May 2, 1957, of a liver ailment. In his last months, he rarely turned up on Capitol Hill, and rumor has it that the bitterness of his defeat, taken with much alcohol, contributed directly to his death.

Senator McCarthy was America's first fatal TV casualty. The power of public opinion, generated by what we the people saw on the nation's TV screens, was too much for this Midwestern demagogue.

The people were watching!

4

Growing Pains

One of the best illustrations of how spot TV developed and matured during the past two decades can be drawn from the progressive changes in video coverage of our presidential conventions during that time. Once every four years, TV faced up to the challenge of bringing to the people the cast and players of a performance that all too often had no script and no logical or predictable ending. TV's coverage of the presidential conventions not only changed radically in the years from 1948 to 1968, but also changed the *nature of the conventions themselves*!

Every nominating convention since the TV age began has been a headache to video broadcasters, even those conventions whose outcome was fairly certain (like the Republican nomination of the Eisenhower-Nixon ticket in 1956 or the Democratic nomination of Lyndon Johnson for president in 1964). The sheer logistics of organizing live coverage of these events — and they must be covered live to preserve their inherent suspense — requiring countless prowling cameramen and announcers, technical crews and "anchor men" for each of the networks, has caused enough confusion to tangle wires and misdeliver cues hundreds of times over the past years.

The networks have tried everything, and, of course, the recent invention of relatively light transistorized TV cameras has made the job of the roving reporter infinitely easier than it was in 1948. In that year the public watched Harry S Truman and Thomas E. Dewey get nominated by the Democrats and Republicans, respectively, from what were largely fixed camera positions. So flexible has TV coverage of conventions now become that party delegates need constantly to be on guard lest a TV camera catch them in embarrassing postures, or talking to the "wrong" party boss, or displaying an unexpected reaction to a nominating speech.

For these reasons, these days the floor of the convention hall has increasingly become less and less of a forum where representatives of a political party get together to discuss how their power is to be deployed in nominating a successful candidate. It has become more and more a showplace, managed by political stage directors who arrange it for the TV audience rather than for the delegates. The actual political maneuvering involved in these occasions—at least, according to such observers as reporter Theodore White and others—is increasingly relegated to corridors, caucus rooms, smoke-filled hotel rooms and even smoke-filled trailer trucks parked outside convention halls.

At the head of the TV team covering political conventions is, of course, the "anchor man," who gives each web's coverage its distinctive flavor. Since 1948, all sorts of people have taken their turn as anchor men: ex-presidents and press secretaries, senators and other assorted polit-

ical types, movie stars and comics. The most successful
have been network political reporters of both experience and skill on the TV medium. These latter tend to fall
into one of two types: "heavies," like Walter Cronkite, the
late Edward R. Murrow, Mike Wallace or Bill Lawrence,
who take their politics seriously; or the brilliant irreverent
funsters, like Dave Brinkley alone or with his partner Chet
Huntley, and John Daly (depending on his mood), who
tend to report conventions as if they were describing the
actions of a hitherto undiscovered tribe of natives in a
weird but complex religious ceremony.

If the convention halls in our great cities presented
problems to broadcasters, they were sometimes relatively
minor compared to the difficulties networks forced on
themselves in the frantic search to discover the kinds of
news shows that might be unique to the TV medium and
which might, somehow, display the peculiar advantages of
the ubiquitous TV camera. At NBC and CBS, they came
up with two different answers, each equally complex in its
own way and each of which tested to the limit the mettle
of their electronic engineers.

NBC developed a concept hatched in the fertile and
unconventional imagination of its one-time executive
Sylvester L. "Pat" Weaver, Jr. To Weaver, TV was an
instrument that tied together immediately, by means of
electronics, and delivered to one's livingroom the wide,
wide world. So Weaver's concept (one of a number of
program formats he originated) was called just that: "Wide
Wide World." It appeared regularly on Sunday afternoons,
a time reserved for "highbrow" or "cultural" programming
in those days. It appeared first on June 27,1955, and then
as a regular on a weekly basis starting October 16, 1955. It
lasted until June 8, 1958, some two years and eight
months, a record that — considering that it was unattractive

to advertisers because of its Sunday time slot and its novel approach — was considerably longer than its detractors had predicted, following its dubious and tentative premiere.

What was "Wide Wide World" exactly? Well, that's difficult to answer, and it is uncertain, in retrospect, whether producer Barry Wood and his subproducers knew either. Each program, or segment of a program, would have an individual theme — say, "Circuses" or the "Symphony of a Great City," "Airplanes" or "Railroads." Then, low-pressure commentator Dave Garroway would begin talking gently about the subject at hand while camera crews across the United States would feed live segments into the program, all more or less coordinated to the major theme. In the later years, presumably having exhausted the limits of live TV in America, the show utilized film from abroad. Each program resembled one big feature newsreel — or a number of little ones — a format which began to wear on the viewers' nerves week after week. "Wide Wide World" was, in its day, however, the ultimate test to which video submitted itself in the massive coordination of numerous on-the-spot broadcasts through one central program, for which the cues were provided by Mr. Garroway and the coordination was activated in one central room.

At CBS, the logistics experts dreamed up a format for Edward R. Murrow which involved a weekly invasion of someone's house or apartment. Murrow himself had little opportunity to display his fullest talents on the program; his job was merely to appear as a charming host and ask a number of carefully rehearsed questions of his "guests." The program was a popular one, never at a loss for advertisers, and it lasted from October 2, 1953, to June 26, 1959, when Murrow left CBS to serve the Federal Government as director of the United States Information Agency in Washington. After some reruns, Charles Collingwood picked up the assignment of hosting "Person to Person" on October 16, 1959, and it finally went off the air on September 15, 1961, a casualty of old age.

The technical ingenuity of "Person to Person" was frequently more amusing and interesting than the interviews themselves. Murrow sat chain-smoking in a studio while he chatted with the TV image of a celebrity whose home, hotel room or temporary residence had been turned into a virtual broadcasting studio by an army of CBS engineers and technicians. The degree of cooperation of Murrow's guests in this weekly invasion of their privacy was extraordinary. Two homes a week were visited for about a quarter of an hour each. Many of Murrow's guests were drawn from the exhibitionist world of show business, but others came from political and cultural fields; occasionally they were not celebrities at all—just a lighthouse operator or school teacher or some other familiar type. So popular was the program that, when Murrow was absent from a CBS studio, his wife, Janet, sometimes conducted the interviews in his place.

As spot TV, "Person to Person" was invariably fascinating live (mostly) TV. Its hidden microphones and ingenious camera placements in every kind of dwelling, from walk-up apartments to baronial mansions, were a constant source of surprise and fun for the alert viewer. The program also managed to maintain a quality of impudent spontaneity, so that when something went wrong—as it often did—and the wrong camera was "punched up" on the screen, or the guest knocked over some of his bric-a-brac, the "fluffs" were graciously integrated by Murrow into his easygoing, conversational format, the tempo and tone of which were never formal or strident.

John F. Kennedy is considered the first "TV president" our nation has known. This is because his victory in 1960 is, in different degrees, attributed by experts to his confrontation in the fall of that year with his Republican opponent, Richard Nixon, on a series of four programs which are today referred to as "The Great Debates." The name is a misnomer; they were not debates in any sense of the term, but rather well-timed and well-stage-managed "interviews" or "press conferences." Whether they were "great" is another question. A review of their transcripts and TV recordings do not vindicate a claim to greatness, at least to us. They seem, instead, to indicate how high-pitched and feverish political sentiments were at the close of the Eisenhower administration and how effectively the medium of TV was able to exploit these sentiments by opposing (or seeming to oppose) two presidential candidates face-to-face. It is generally agreed, however, that whatever the broadcasts were, Kennedy appeared more competent and articulate than his rival, Nixon, on TV.

The Kennedy administration lasted the approximate "thousand days" that have, in the short half decade since, become a period of legends. They made up a short segment of history when Washington — not New York — appeared to be the social and cultural center of the nation. The executive branch of our government gave personal — and well-publicized — attention to the arts, literature and the academic community, and President Kennedy himself seemed continually aware and appreciative of the TV medium that had been so instrumental in his election. His press conferences were televised in their entirety, live and directly from the White House. He unquestionably used his own telegenic appeal to advantage when he broadcast his speeches to the people over the TV medium. Rather than require a celebrated "TV adviser," like his predecessor President Eisenhower, Kennedy himself possessed a sense of showmanship that rivaled the skill of any and all professionals he selected to coach him on the use of TV to communicate with the people.

The President was not the only member of his personal family who recognized the power of the medium to bring together, more closely than ever before in history, the executive arm of government and the people. Kennedy's charming wife, Jacqueline, agreed to conduct a televised tour of the White House in 1962, explaining to the people the delightful project to which she had set herself as First Lady: the restoration of the interior of the building as a national shrine, a living museum of the American Presidency.

Mrs. Kennedy was (and is) a person of considerable natural poise and charm, and, accompanied by veteran announcer Charles Collingwood, this unique on-the-spot telecast was taped and then broadcast on February 14, 1962. Mrs. Kennedy and Collingwood chatted informally about the various rooms of the building, many of which were in the process of restoration and, for the final minutes of the telecast, were joined by the President himself, who expressed appreciation for the interest that his wife and others were taking in the development of this beautiful living memorial to the many presidents who had resided in the historic building on Pennsylvania Avenue in Washington.

Mrs. Kennedy was by no means a TV "natural" on a par with her husband, but graciously wearing low-heeled shoes out of deference to Collingwood's small stature, she carried off the occasion with surprising ease.

Here was a fine example of spot TV covering — not hard news, but an aspect of our national heritage of great interest to millions of American adults and children. It was a type of TV experiment never before — or since — attempted with quite the same success.

The Kennedy years ended abruptly in the early afternoon, as almost every American alive at the time knows, of Friday, November 22, 1963, at Dallas, Texas, when an assassin's rifle bullet pierced the skull of John Fitzgerald Kennedy, killing him almost immediately.

On NBC-TV, the announcement was read over the audio portion of the TV network: "President Kennedy," it said, "was shot in Dallas, Texas, today. Blood was seen on the President's head as they rushed him to the hospital. Mrs. Kennedy was heard to exclaim, 'Oh, no!'" Just that.

The announcement was correct as far as it went, and from that afternoon until early the following Tuesday morning, the nation was figuratively glued to its TV sets watching on-the-spot coverage of a type that had never before been attempted anywhere in the world and proved irrefutably that American TV could respond to the challenge of covering significant action with a profundity and clarity never before achieved by any news medium. How ironic that a president had to be killed to prove the obvious!

First, all regular programs were canceled, and the commercial announcements were shelved for the occasion. These two moves were demanded by the solemnity of the event. The news staffs of both networks were alerted immediately to give total coverage of the transfer of government to the Vice-President, Lyndon Johnson, and the subsequent funeral of President Kennedy in Washington.

Books have been written about the days, even the hours, that were to follow, but nothing has been written which can begin to recapture the emotions of the American public, who literally became eyewitnesses to the incredible unfolding of history that occurred in Dallas, Texas, and Washington, D.C., in the ensuing days.

What do we remember most clearly in the mind's eye: the arrest of the alleged slayer, Lee Harvey Oswald? Scenes of the survivors arriving at Andrews Air Force Base? That first short interview with Lee Harvey Oswald? The faces of the mourners, whose expressions somehow combined incredulity, numbness and grief? The lines of mourners who filed past President Kennedy's casket as he lay in state, guarded by members of the Armed Forces in formal uniforms? The funeral itself, on Monday, as the procession made its mournfully slow way, to the sounds of drum beats and horses' hooves, down the wide streets of Washington to St. Matthew's cathedral, site of the funeral?

So meaningful were these images, caught sensitively by corps of TV cameramen and narrated with fine dignity and restraint by newcasters, that they blur in one's memory, tempered only by deep feelings of participation in the sorry events of this tragic weekend, feelings directly resulting from the magnificent TV coverage provided by our broadcasters. The seers who pronounce the arbitrary viewer statistics by which telecasters unfortunately live (and by which their programs also live) estimate that between ninety and one hundred million Americans watched the omnibus coverage of the events of that weekend. Possibly the statistic is accurate.

At exactly 12:20 P.M. on Sunday, November 24, an event also occurred in front of the network live TV cameras which was so incredible that many of us, even after countless tape replays, could not believe our eyes or ears.

Lee Harvey Oswald, the then suspected killer of the President, was about to be transferred from the Dallas city jail to the Dallas county jail, where, supposedly, security would be superior and where, under the law, he belonged. Suddenly, those of us in the TV audience saw a stocky man in a dark suit wearing a light fedora detach himself from the crowd of onlookers and run towards Oswald. The latter, wearing a sweater and an open sport shirt, was well guarded and flanked on either side by detectives. We suddenly noticed that the man in the fedora was carrying a gun. At close range, and with what seems, on careful inspection, to be more than amateur skill, the stocky man fired directly into the upper abdomen of Lee Harvey Oswald. Here is Tom Petit's eyewitness account of the event, which was heard (and seen) by millions of televiewers.

"He's been shot! He's been shot! He's been shot! Lee Oswald has been shot. There's a man with a gun! There's absolute panic, absolute panic here in the basement of the Dallas Police Headquarters. Detectives have their guns drawn. Oswald has been shot. There's no question about it. Oswald has been shot. Pandemonium has broken loose here in the basement of Dallas Police Headquarters!"

This was network TV, covering, on the spot, the murder of Kennedy's accused assassin by gambler Jack Ruby with an entire nation in the audience!

Recently, the authors of this book had replayed for them a long series of tapes and films of the Oswald murder, exhibited in private in the plush comfort of a viewing room at the headquarters of one of the networks in New York City. We spent the entire morning viewing and re-viewing the episode in every version the network's archives contained. We studied piles of still pictures and yards of film and tape in the unspoken anticipation that perhaps just one more look, in the perspective of events in the half-decade since that afternoon, might miraculously give us a key to the solution of a mystery that will probably never be solved.

The most remarkable live TV coverage ever made, preserved now for history on tape and film, will keep its secret, we think, forever!

But then, we thought, how foolish! That weekend in November contained but one tragedy: the death of our

President, whom TV had brought so close to all of us when he was alive. And we remembered how, with an entire nation, we mourned his death in silent vigil before our TV receivers on that fearful weekend in November not so long ago.

ABC-TV: Washington

Washington correspondents, not only for TV but also for radio and newspapers, will tell you with a straight face that Washington, D.C., is the news capital of the country—of the world, in fact, if they are feeling expansive. It isn't! But it is the political capital of the United States of America, and a lot of news is made there in the various government bureaus and news agencies, in political party headquarters, on Capitol Hill, in the Supreme Court, in the Senate and House of Representatives and especially in the White House.

From the news perspective, the Washington beat centers on one star performer and more supporting players than any reporter can keep in mind at one time. The star is the President of the United States, whose executive power probably exceeds that of anyone on earth, and the power focuses on one famous building on Pennsylvania Avenue: the White House. Presidents may vacation in Florida, camp in the mountains or run the "goodwill" circuit through South America and Europe; but they come to live in the great mansion with the flawless lawns, the impeccable flowerbeds and more than a century and a half of American history built into its bedrooms, offices, pictures and furniture.

Everett Aspinwall, the acting head of the American Broadcasting Company's Washington bureau, is only slightly less enthusiastic than the average D.C. newsman. He will candidly admit that only about 40 percent of our national TV news originates from the nation's capital, most of it on film. Everett himself would never be mistaken for a Washingtonian, for his speech is almost pure New England. It is no surprise to discover that he hails from Rhode Island and that he is a graduate of Dartmouth, a bastion of New England rectitude for centuries, who began his broadcasting career at the university's radio station as an undergraduate in the early 1950s.

"I took my B.A. in chemistry, oddly enough," Ev told us. "My family is in the textile-chemistry business, and I fully intended to follow in my hereditary footsteps. Or so I thought when I got my M.A. at North Carolina State in textiles. Within a couple of years I was in the radio business, though—let's see—in Newton, New Jersey, Worcester, Massachusetts, and Portland, Maine. From the beginning I was at the news desk. I guess my lucky break came in 1958 when CBS hired me as a news writer and I moved to New York. Then off I went to ABC news in Chicago in 1964. From there my future as a bureau chief developed."

Everett, a dark-haired, serious-looking, mature and highly affable man, leaned back in his swivel chair. "I hate to think that I've made good on the misfortunes of others, but my major assignment in Chicago was the great Alaska earthquake of March 27, 1964. The Chicago news bureau handled much of that story for ABC's radio and TV networks. Then, almost two years later to the day, I was reassigned here to Washington as bureau manager of TV news. One job just led naturally to another."

The Washington bureau, Everett explained, employs about 120 people and prepares news stories and clips for ABC network news shows and documentaries. "We have what we call the DEF, the daily electronic feed to the network every day at 5 P.M. That is, we send out over the lines four or five stories to the network which New York and all the affiliates receive," said Everett.

"The bureau chief is John Lynch here in Washington, who happens to be on vacation this month, and I'm acting for him. Ordinarily, I'm manager of TV news.

"There are thirteen correspondents at the Washington bureau. Some of them are general-assignment reporters. Some are as well known as Edward P. Morgan (now on leave to Public Television), Howard K. Smith and Joseph C. Harsh. Some correspondents have definite beats which they cover daily: John Scali at the State Department, Frank Reynolds at the White House, Bob Clark on Capitol Hill, Bill Downs at the Pentagon and Bill Lawrence the political beat. For instance, Frank Reynolds will be at the White House and will attend the daily 11 A.M. and 4 P.M. briefings held by Press Secretary George Christian. He'll be briefed along with the others on what the President's business for the day is, who he is seeing and where he is going. Wherever the President goes in this country or abroad, Frank Reynolds will go too.

"The individual correspondent is the brain of the TV news team and its nerve center as well. Each of them is backed up by one of six camera crews, consisting of a camera and sound man and an electrician when their coverage is on motion picture film. Once the raw film — always

in color these days—has been shot, it is rushed by courier
on a motorbike (to speed through Washington's eternal
daytime traffic snarl) to be processed in the ABC laboratory by Erdman Reck and his staff in a new semiautomated
color motion picture film developer."

"The trick," Everett continued, "is to shoot footage of
national importance and get it onto network news programs by 5:30 P.M. On a good day—and if we're lucky
—that means that we can film an interview in color on
Capitol Hill as late as 4:00 P.M. and still make our deadline, if everything works right, and sometimes it does!"
He held up a pair of crossed fingers.

Everett Aspinwall continued, "If you ask about TV tape
or live coverage, that's another problem, and, at the
present—I mean August, 1967—'problem' is exactly the
word, because film is still a heck of a lot more flexible than
tape or live TV for network news coverage. First of all,
we have lines provided by the telephone company for
direct coverage from locations in the city, like the Capitol
and the White House. The three networks operate the
White House TV theater on a pooled basis all year round.
That means that an ABC staff will telecast press conferences for a few months, then NBC, then CBS, dividing the
cost in this manner. News conferences held in the famous
East Room of the White House can also be televised in
this way; the same with the President's office. Each network then broadcasts its coverage directly or saves it on
tape and edits it as it wishes. We put everything else we
get from the White House on film."

"Things are a little different over on 'the Hill,'" explained Everett, using the ubiquitous Washington nick-
name for the Capitol building. "Over there, we have a
Senate radio-TV press gallery set up for filming, and all
networks have access to it. We also have remote live lines

for tape coverage, but, since our cameras are not allowed on the floor of Congress, a lot of what we broadcast from the Hill comes from on-the-spot interviews conducted in the lobbies or outside a hearing room or anywhere we can collar a Senator or Representative. Film is obviously best for this kind of interview. You've probably noticed this 'catch-as-catch-can' coverage on your own sets. Of course, we're allowed access to certain House and Senate hearings; the most famous were the Army-McCarthy hearings in the 1950s. When we do this kind of live coverage, or even tape live coverage in a mobile unit or on recorders here at the studios, we are usually involved in a pool operation with the other networks for production. Incidentally, we also pool with the other nets for coverage of the White House Ranch in Texas. KONO-TV in San Antonio, Texas, is the ABC affiliate that always covers presidential news conferences in Texas. The three networks have given equipment to the station for this purpose."

"Money is a central problem in covering news by TV," continued Everett. "That's the simple reason why networks use pools so much—that and the fact that three networks covering one event create a snarl of cameras and personnel. But look here—now, these figures are only approximate—when the networks cover a White House press conference, what do you think it costs them, say with *one* color mobile unit?" The question was rhetorical. "About $3,000. A slightly bigger job with five cameras—what I'd call respectable coverage—runs $11,500 or so. Now, to cover something live or on tape like the launching of a battleship can run to $30,000. That's not hay, even considering the network pool, which cuts ABC's costs to a third. Look, I'm not crying poverty, but you know as well as I do that news shows do not attract advertisers and make money the way entertainment shows do. In fact, their story can be written in red ink, even though news coverage is, in my opinion—and yours too, probably—the most important thing a TV station broadcasts! Well, ABC's news coverage in Washington costs them somewhere between $80,000 and $150,000 per year."

"Big remotes cost big money," said Everett. "Take President Johnson's trip to Punta del Este in Uruguay recently. Here's how we handled it: three months in advance of the announced conference, a unit manager and I made an initial survey trip to Uruguay to look over the site of the conference, to decide what kind of coverage to give (live or film), to line up support facilities, to rent hotel rooms and automobiles and to hire office help and interpreters and bilingual chauffers locally. We then returned to the bureau headquarters in Washington and made a formal proposal to the New York office. In New York they decided what we would be permitted to do—because the purse strings are in New York. However, Washington handles it because it is a presidential story.

"After New York approval, we went back to Punta to nail down and hire all the help and facilities we needed now that we had the budget in hand. Also, we did some advance filming of local color, of fill shots, of the building of a new hall for the conference, of removing machines from a gambling casino to make more room for the conference. We also covered Secretary of State Dean Rusk, who was there to develop the agenda for the conference. Then the main contingent came in with the President.

"In the Punta conference, we went strictly with film because the satellite was not in correct position for live transmission to the States. Although the flight schedules out of Punta were not too good, we managed to fly our film out to the States with enough speed. We used five film crews and approximately eighty-five people. We left when

the President left. The cost to ABC for about three weeks
was $200,000. Three news specials were made out of the
action we covered. And we didn't get all our money back."

Ev was on his feet now, serious and intense. "You want
to know the inside story of televised spot news? Well, this
is the viewpoint from the bureau chief's desk: on the network level, spot news is spot news, and when it breaks,
whether the financial officers of our corporations like it or
not, we've *got* to cover it if it is humanly possible, and the
money involved is irrelevant. Mainly, you've got to get the
story and forget your checkbook. The Kennedy assassina-
tion and funeral were examples. Or take the so-called race
riots this summer; they presented a thousand delicate
problems, but the TV networks had to cover them. When
news breaks, I can charter a plane and send a crew anywhere within the realm of my bureau, and so can our other
chiefs in the other ABC bureaus around the world. And I
will, if an important enough scoop comes through that door
or over the phone this minute. This is the kind of TV
coverage — and it makes no difference whether its on tape
or film or live — that only a network can provide: coverage
of continuing spot news wherever it happens and at whatever the cost. This is what ABC tries to do. Like our competitors, we don't always succeed, but I think our record is
enviable and comparable with theirs! We have bureaus in
Washington, D.C., Chicago, Atlanta, Los Angeles and
Miami in the States, and in London, Paris, Rome, Moscow, Hong Kong and Saigon abroad. New York is not
considered a bureau, it is home office. In addition,
throughout the world we have 215 stringers, 150 of which
are in the United States."

Everett Aspinwall's New England calm had been disturbed. He chuckled. "I make it all sound more dramatic
than it is, I guess, but in this business you remember the

drama and forget the routine." "Incidentally," he added, "this news bureau here on Connecticut Avenue belongs to the network. It has little to do with our Washington affiliate, WMAL-TV, that's housed a couple of miles up the avenue. Of course, we work closely with the local station, but this is a network operation entirely; our orders come from headquarters in New York — as do directives to all the other ABC bureaus around the world. On a day-to-day basis, this entire building — and the one we're moving into next door as well — has the primary responsibility of making inserts into ABC's half-hour news programs. That, and our radio broadcasts. For this sort of operation, we are well equipped, as you can see."

There is plenty for the visitor to look at in ABC's Washington news headquarters. Besides a newsroom, offices and secretarial space, the building boasts two color TV studios, a complete film processing unit, four color video tape recorders, color film chains (instruments by which sound film is introduced into a TV broadcast), four film editing rooms for four editors and two screening rooms (small motion picture theaters). A few studio programs originate weekly from the ABC studios, either live or on tape, but most telecasts that ABC sends from its news building on Connecticut Avenue are on motion picture film, shot by a correspondent and film crew, edited with sound and with narration added by the correspondent and subsequently fed to New York City, where the network disseminates it to its numerous affiliates.

After the tour, Everett turned to us. "If you are interested in spot TV news, the fellow you should meet is Dick Saunders. He's working our assignment desk for TV this morning, and he can give you more details about what's up in the 'district' today than I can." (The "district" is what Washington newsmen call their beat: the District of Columbia and its environs in neighboring Maryland and Virginia.) "But let's have lunch first. Duke Zeibert's restaurant is just around the corner, and it's a hangout for a lot of Washington news types and also some of the people who make the news."

The restaurant, except for the "good-to-see-you-again" handclasp of the proprietor, was indistinguishable from any other Broadway-style restaurant, but it was packed with Washington correspondents and speedy waiters. Ev and we ate with two local TV reporters, public-relations man Heywood Meeks of WMAL-TV and gravel-voiced veteran Washington correspondent Bill Lawrence. The latter was overflowing with enthusiasm for a political feature show on the coming elections he had just completed for ABC. "A couple of days in New York to clear up things, and then to Portland, Maine and New Hampshire." Lawrence was asked why Maine and New Hampshire. He answered with a wink. "Political news goes everywhere. 'As Maine goes, so goes the nation' — remember? And they run state primary elections for the presidency in New Hampshire. Of course, it's an off year and the middle of the summer, but I just might come up with something interesting on film." Some of us, including Ev, looked dubious, but the rest of the luncheon guests appeared to agree with Lawrence.

Back in ABC's newsroom, we met Dick Saunders, ABC's Washington assignment editor. For a man whose job is the logistics of a TV news bureau and whose telephones never stop ringing, Dick, mostly because of his soft voice and diffident manner, offers a first impression of almost painful shyness. This is a false picture, dispelled almost entirely as soon as you see him in command of the four telephones (which are sometimes used two at a clip) and microphones to two-way radio in TV remote units on his desk, three TV sets which are tuned to the major networks and the piles of wire service copy which passes across his desk. While Dick is in charge of the TV Assignment Desk, John Gallagher, a red-haired youngster, veteran of five years at ABC, takes care of radio assignments and gives Dick a hand when the going gets rough.

"My background?" replied Dick to a question. "I'll tell you about it if the phones stop ringing long enough — or if you can keep up with what I say between calls." A phone rang, and Dick was discussing an interview planned with a Senator in a Capitol hallway. With camera crew and correspondent all set, the Senator had sprung a toothache and gone to his dentist. Dick Saunders was calm in the face of crisis; he was obviously talking to the correspondent assigned to the interview, "Well look, you're all set up. Why don't you interview *another* Senator? What about what's-his-name, Senator Toothache's sidekick? Try to interview *somebody*, huh? They want some footage from 'the Hill' on the show tonight. Good boy!" He cradled the phone thoughtfully and murmured, "A toothache!"

"Now, what is my background?" mused Dick. "In a nutshell, I was born in Chicago, graduated from the University of Missouri Journalism School in 1950. I had gotten some news experience on the Columbia station WTPS and then on to New Orleans, Spartanburg, South Carolina, and Jackson, Mississippi, for twelve years. I've been here in Washington for two years; I'm married and the father of two sons, fifteen and thirteen. I doubt that either of them will want to go into TV broadcasting, and I personally would rather they found something more — well — steady, but frankly it's up to them and — " a phone rang — "excuse me."

More problems on Capitol Hill. Dick remained calm and made another call. Evidently his correspondent had found a Senator to interview.

"No," he said, turning back to us, "whatever the boys do

is their business, eventually, I suppose, although my wife would like them to have a more normal life. Today I'll work eight hours — the fates willing — but I may be on this desk ten, twelve or even sixteen hours, depending on how the news breaks. I've been called at home to assign crews and correspondents to cover stories at two o'clock in the morning. You see, only the assignment editor knows where the various camera crews are and where the personnel can be reached. I may send a remote unit from Washington to the Pentagon, or, if a crew is needed somewhere else, I may release one assigned somewhere in Virginia covering a feature story to get some film footage on a story breaking in their vicinity. Any kind of story, from an interview to a tornado! This job boils down to logistics mostly — and judgment, and experience. You have to know what's more important than what — and the kind of — footage on film or tape or what kind of live remote TV setup the ABC network people in New York are going to want. If you can't guess 'em right, you don't belong at the assignment desk."

In between phone calls, interruptions, trips to Ev Aspinwall's office for advice and paper work, Dick explained that the "district" had certain "beats" that had to be covered, like the Capitol when the House of Representatives or the Senate or both are in session, the White House when the President is there and various government departments that are likely to be in the news. The rest of his job, Dick noted, consisted of watching what he called "the pattern of the news" develop in Washington day by day and, like moving pieces on a checker board, making certain that it was being covered somehow — and in color — by ABC film or TV cameras.

"Nothing is certain at this desk. Right now, a number of important things are happening here in Washington. The

Senate is holding hearings on the riot emergency. They *must* think that's important because Senators hate the Washington summer heat. Something is up at the White House. I don't know what, but the President is entertaining an important head of a foreign state. Other events are in the works that just *might* lead me to take for granted that the network will use two or three Washington news stories on tonight's TV news shows. On the other hand, floods are breaking in Fairbanks, Alaska, and *that* may be where the news is. One flood, one earthquake or one foreign uprising can wipe Washington from the TV screen. Remember that the average ABC affiliate devotes one-half an hour at a time to news, and if too much is happening in too many places, something has to give. And that something may be a news story we've carefully cultivated here in Washington for days!"

With a shrug, Dick picked up a large book like an accountant's ledger and opened it. The pages were filled with entries in pen and pencil. "We call this our 'futures book,' and it represents the best guess I can make about what stories our people will be out on in the near future." Dick began turning the pages. "Take tomorrow, for instance," he said.

Suddenly, he smiled. "Now I have a notation here that tomorrow the President may — mind you, I said *may* — meet the press for some kind of news conference." He slammed the book shut and looked straight at us. "This may be a bit tricky, but I think Ev may be able to arrange it — and I'm not guaranteeing anything — but, tomorrow, how would you two fellows like to join our man at the White House and get a firsthand look at how television covers the President of the the United States in person?"

6

TV at the White House

Official notice came from the President's press staff by phone and made the wire services seconds later the following morning shortly before 10:00 A.M. Chancellor Kurt Georg Kiesinger of the Federal Republic of West Germany, who had been welcomed to Washington the previous evening, and President Johnson would hold a meeting (and possibly a press conference) in the south garden of the White House promptly at 2:00 that afternoon. The press was invited, and that meant TV coverage by film.

The date was Tuesday, August 15, 1967, and, if all you had to do was sightseeing, Washington was at its loveliest. The temperature was near 90 degrees, and lines of tourists outside the White House snapped interminable photographs of the stately mansion; trios of flags (that of the United States, West Germany and the District of Columbia) were fluttering from every lamppost surrounding the President's home, and, with the sun at high noon, you hardly cast a shadow as you crossed Lafayette Park to Pennsylvania Avenue.

As good as their word, Dick Saunders and Everett Aspinwall had arranged for us to join the correspondents at the White House that afternoon, thanks to the kindness of Robert Fleming, one of the President's Deputy Press Secretaries. Having arrived early at the White House (our appointment with Dan Hackel, ABC's assistant White House correspondent, who was covering the regular beat for Frank Reynolds, was set for 12:30), we walked once around the mansion and the executive offices adjacent to it and past Blair House, where Chancellor Kiesinger and his party were housed, with its phalanx of chauffered, official-looking black automobiles lined up in front. The walk was longer and harder than we had expected, and we ended up, overheated and still early, eating popsicles on a park bench not one hundred feet from the northwest gate, where, we were told, we were "expected." We were not sure just who expected us.

Dick Saunders had warned that we might not even get to see the President, that the meeting might be canceled. "In that case," he assured us, "you'll see a lot of disappointed correspondents — and some mad ones too." We agreed that this would be all right with us, and so there we sat, in the boiling sun, waiting for our watches to move slowly from 12:25 to 12:30, eating popsicles. What we did not know was that we were to spend another *two hours* in that same sun as the temperature mounted — and without popsicles or benches to sit on!

Two White House guards in a hut just off the avenue listened suspiciously to our story, made a few phone calls and then directed us down a gravel path to the west lobby, known as the "press lobby," of the executive mansion. We asked if we needed some sort of tag or identification. One

guard smiled. "We know you're here. Just go ahead in."
We did.

The press lobby, or "lounge," itself is spacious, fur-
nished with comfortable green leather chairs and comfortably air-conditioned. A clublike atmosphere pervaded the
large room where reporters read newspapers, snoozed but
mostly talked to one another. A number of abstract paintings hung on either side of the lounge and, completely out
of place on the far wall, reposed a full-size reproduction of
Gilbert Stuart's portrait of George Washington. To the
right, a small room was filled with ticker tapes, a soft-drink
machine, a water fountain and bemused reporters in small
groups. Nearby are the offices of Presidential Press Secretary George Christian and his deputies. We were reminded by Irwin Chapman, one of the ABC News Bureau
correspondents, who cautioned us, before we left ABC
bureau headquarters on Connecticut Avenue, of the ground
rules that pertained in these press facilities. "You cannot
record on film, tape (audio or video), or take still photographs inside these premises. If you want to have an on-
the-record press conference, you have to invite your guest
outside and record it there. Inside, you can use a pencil
and paper to record a press conference. Someday the
electronic media may achieve equality." We asked for Dan
Hackel of ABC.

Hackel introduced himself and immediately apologized.
"The man you really want to write about in this book of
yours is Frank Reynolds, but he's in New York doing the
Peter Jennings news spot. Jennings is vacationing, and so
you're stuck here at the White House with me!"

Such, we explained to Hackel, a dark, obviously eager
and bright young man of about 30, was the way the wheels
of fate rolled. We sat down together in a small cluster of
green armchairs, cool and comfortable.

"I consider taking over this beat from Reynolds, even temporarily, a real break." Dan told us about his education, his graduation from the Columbia University School of Journalism in New York, his service in the Air Force, his apprenticeship with WEWS, the ABC affiliate in Cleveland, and the opportunity he had to set up the first English-language newsroom in Puerto Rico for station WTSJ in San Juan. Hackel had been with ABC in Washington for only a year, and he kept insisting that Reynolds was really the man we wanted to interview. From the lounge we walked together to ABC's broadcasting booth, a tiny room next to the row of teletype machines.

"In this room," explained Dan, "we can make direct audio contact with the studios. We can also telephone from here and store our equipment, but not much more. In my opinion, the White House is a pretty restrictive place for a TV newsman — or any newsman, for that matter. While we're physically pretty close to the President — his office is just beyond that wall — we're as far away from him as his press secretary, George Christian, or the President himself wants us to be. Over there, incidentally, is the 'Fish Room,' which is used for briefing correspondents concerning the President's daily activities. It's called the Fish Room because when Franklin Roosevelt was president, stuffed fish were hung on its walls. The fish disappeared, but the name stuck. The same thing is true of the garden, where you'll see the President this afternoon. It's called the Rose Garden, but there are no roses in it. You'll see a lot of flowers but not a rosebush. The White House staff tries to call it the South Garden, but it is still the Rose Garden to these correspondents. That's the way things are here in the White House. Many of the press corps have been here longer than the last four presidents combined, and they don't change their ways quickly."

In ABC's broadcasting booth we met Al Recht, an audio engineer on his way to lunch, and Gene Brandus tuning up a tape recorder. "I guess I'll be with you in the garden," said Gene. "Bob Hemmig is on camera and probably out there setting up already. He and an audio technician will be taking color movies of the meeting, or conference, or whatever it's supposed to be. I think we have a hot afternoon ahead of us!" he said ominously.

"Why don't you fellows go on out into the garden? They're calling for the still photographers now," added Dan Hackel. "You want to see them set up, don't you? I'll come out later when the correspondents are called for, and I'll join you then."

We asked Dan Hackel what the President and Chancellor Kiesinger were likely to say. Dan shrugged. "Who knows? The President might drop a bomb—something about America and Germany uniting against the Arabs in the Near East, but I doubt it. He might have something to say about France or West Germany's relations with East Germany. My guess might be that both the President and the Chancellor will affirm their friendship etc., etc., etc., but I don't like to guess! Anyway, we'll know in less than an hour; it's already after one! That is, if the conference is on time."

The Rose Garden was a hive of activity, although everyone was cautioned to make as little noise as possible. At one end a set of garden furniture was placed among the bushes. No one had nerve enough to use it, however; it was obviously reserved for the President's family. A hedge surrounded the rest of the garden, over one side of which hung a portico casting a feeble shadow, where we attempted to find refuge during the ensuing hours. At the other end of a magnificent lawn was a porch leading directly to large glass doors curtained off from one of the

White House's many reception rooms. On the porch, a rostrum had been placed bearing the Great Seal of the President of the United States. A row of movie cameramen were setting up their instruments on aluminum and plywood platforms in the center of the garden. An area with a radius of about ten feet had been chained off in front of the rostrum, obviously intended to prevent any reporters from getting too near the President and the Chancellor. A group of still photographers were ushered into the garden and allowed to focus their cameras, and then they were herded out, back to the press lounge.

White House guards in their navy-blue trousers and white shirts and side arms in leather holsters paraded along the side patio. American Secret Servicemen, trying hard to look as if they had something to do, kept their eyes on the cameramen and audio technicians — and us! The German guards present were more noticeable; each wore a lapel pin and appeared grim. Nearly everyone was perspiring by the time that half an hour passed. The cameramen removed their jackets, but the German and American bodyguards (for reasons best known to their trade) kept theirs on. So did we, and by now our shirts were soaked.

The sun was getting so warm that nearly all the audio engineers moved their recorders from the direct sunlight into the shade cast by their wooden tables. Absurd-looking parasols sprouted one after the other like colored mushrooms over the motion picture cameras. We asked a worried Bob Hemmig, ABC's cameraman, about the parasols. "I wish the President would hurry — not for my sake, but for the film's," he replied. "We're shooting in color, and heat effects the emulsion on the film. The parasol may cool the cameras down a bit — at least, we hope so. I'm shooting sound film — that is, color film with a magnetic sound strip. Another ABC cameraman — Carl Lawsen — is on the roof shooting cover-shots silent. That means he's taking silent footage from a hand-held camera to set the scene and add some variety to my film — which can just move from medium shots of both speakers at the rostrum to close-ups by using this zoom lens. That is, if the sun doesn't ruin my film!"

At precisely 2:00 P.M., the correspondents filed in. We joined Dan Hackel for a hushed conversation. "Still no guess!" said Hackel, and we moved to the center of the lawn with the rest of the correspondents, a half-dozen of them women, behind the roped-off area; the rostrum was twelve feet away. Behind us, the still photographers were stationed, their cameras held above our heads; behind them stood the motion picture photographers on their platforms; and behind them and to the side were the audio engineers and technicians, quietly waiting and mopping their brows in the summer heat. Other still and motion picture photographers with hand-held cameras were stationed on the roof of the portico.

Half an hour later, at 2:30, everyone was still waiting. The reporters were quipping with each other, and one veteran White House correspondent sat down unhappily on the grass. "What on earth did we say about *him* now, that *he* is getting even by broiling us in the sun?" muttered one lady reporter to no one. "My feet hurt!" said another attractive lady reporter. Dan Hackel was deep in conversation with two of his colleagues.

At 2:32 exactly, the curtains on the glass doors moved, the door opened, and out stepped President Lyndon B. Johnson and Chancellor Kurt G. Kiesinger. They made their way briskly to the rostrum while an assortment of German and American aides formed a line behind them on the porch. The aides all looked recently well fed and happy. Johnson, wearing a blue shirt, blue suit and red-striped tie, seemed sunburned and fit. Chancellor Kiesinger, a dignified continental gentleman with long gray hair, was also dressed in navy blue but sported a white shirt, less favored than blue by TV and film cameramen. The reporters began scratching notes. Cameras started whirring, and the clicks of the still cameras sounded like a hundred baby crickets learning to crick.

Neither the Chancellor nor the President spoke from notes. Johnson, in his quiet Texan drawl, observed that he and the Chancellor had had a successful meeting and discussed matters of mutual interest, and that he looked forward to entertaining Kiesinger and his party further. Kiesinger, speaking in English, echoed Johnson's sentiments, indicated how cordial he had found his Washington reception and commented on some of West Germany's problems, which he was sure President Johnson understood. Then, without another word, the President, the Chancellor and their aides slipped back through the glass doors into the White House. End of event! It was 2:39 P.M.

The correspondents looked more frustrated than furious. "Not a question!" snapped one. "He didn't let us ask a single question. What kind of press conference was this?" Others grumbled silently as Dan Hackel joined us in our walk through the press lounge to the ABC broadcasting booth. Dan looked grim. "Do you see now why I don't like guessing what the President will do? At least we can be sure of one thing; it's doubtful whether the U.S.A. and Germany will declare war on one another within the next twelve hours! Right now I've got to call Bruce Cohn, my producer at the studio."

Once inside the booth, Dan was on a direct line to the ABC studios. He explained exactly what had occurred in the Rose Garden. The time was 2:45, just twenty-three minutes after the President had stepped to the rostrum. "Look, Bruce," said Dan into the phone, "obviously neither man wanted to expose himself to questions under those conditions. It was a goodwill gesture. But I think we can take, say, thirty seconds or so of each speech and some cover shots, as well as the welcoming footage we shot last night to make a two-minute segment for New York — that is, if they want it. Anyway, I'll write my narration — about a minute altogether, huh?" Dan obviously received an affirmative answer. Then he turned to us.

"If you fellows hot-foot it back to ABC, you'll get there by the time the film of the speeches is developed. It left here ten minutes ago, by the way, so don't hurry. See Bruce Cohn there, and you'll find out what becomes of it."

After a soda and a few minutes' rest in the air-conditioned press lounge, we were back on Pennsylvania Avenue, a little cooler now but still tangled with traffic at 3:35. We made our way to Connecticut Avenue and back to the ABC studios. Shortly after 4:00, we discovered Bruce Cohn, a thin, energetic young man of 36, in his shirt sleeves, waiting for the processed film from the White House to be delivered from the lab to a viewing room. "New York says Dan will have to settle for one minute and forty-five seconds, like it or not, on the Johnson-Kiesinger meeting. You guys were there, I hear." We nodded. "Pretty dull, huh?" We found ourselves running after Cohn to a viewing room. "Take a look," he said, "and see what you saw."

On the screen ran the sum total of Bob Hemmig's efforts. The colors were clear, and the camera moved artfully from Johnson to Kiesinger and back again. The sound was flawless. In fact, both voices sounded better in the viewing room than on the White House lawn. Bruce Cohn was on his feet. "If you want to see how this busi-

ness works, why don't you join Ed Stern in the cutting
room right now. Our deadline is 5:30, and we've got less
than an hour to get this and another show together and
transmit them to New York. We can talk afterwards."
Cohn disappeared, and we found ourselves in a tiny cutting room with six other people cheek by jowl. Ed Stern,
the film cutter, was selecting film from two reels: one, Bob
Hemmig's sound footage that we had just seen, and the
other, the silent film made from the roof of the portico.
Clips taken the night before were pinned like drying laun-
dry to a frame on Ed's left. Assistants were making notes
and helping Ed select the clips.

Deftly, by looking at the moviola in front of him, by
listening to the sound track and by hunch, Ed Stern first
patched together and then cemented a small reel of
film—just one minute and forty-five seconds of running
time. An assistant was writing down a description of the
shots and sound cues for transmittal to New York and for
the record. No sooner had a few of the occupants of the
cutting room disappeared in what was developing into a
feverish race against the clock (that now read 5:15) than
Bruce Cohn and Dan Hackel appeared. "Look, Dan,"
pleaded Bruce, "can't you cut your narration by five seconds? Or maybe speed it up." Hackel scratched his head
and read his short introduction (to be read over the silent
clips) and his final summation (to cover the final handshake
and exit of the President and the Chancellor). Bruce Cohn
looked unhappy. "That last part still needs cutting," he
said.

"I'll get it yet!" said Dan Hackel, writing as he hurried
down the hall, shaking his head.

The minutes went by with unbelievable speed. At 5:29,
we found ourselves in the master control room with about
thirteen other people, including four attractive girls who

seemed to have arrived from nowhere and whose presence was not explained. We were about to ask who they were when the TV monitors in front of us — at least a dozen of them — and the receiver on which we were leaning exploded with the information, in full color, that *Peter Jennings with the news was on the air* and that tonight Frank Reynolds was substituting for him. Bruce Cohn buried his face in his hands, the picture of a man whose future was now in the hands of fate.

The news show proceeded along smoothly enough for a few minutes, and then Reynolds in New York said, ". . . and now for a report on today's meeting between Chancellor Kiesinger and President Johnson, we switch to ABC in Washington." At the words "Chancellor Kiesinger" everyone in the control room sat bolt upright. Dan Hackel's voice filled the room with his introduction; then came a few words from President Johnson and a few from Chancellor Kiesinger. Hackel's closing statement was just the right length and finished as the silent film ended. The picture on the TV tubes returned to Frank Reynolds in New York.

"What a business!" said Bruce Cohn later in his office. "I went to school and trained on the West Coast — San Francisco and Los Angeles — but it's the same everywhere. First I was a writer. Now I'm an assistant producer, and I hope someday I'll be a producer, like I was tonight. I'm on this assignment now because our regular man is on vacation. But TV is a team effort anyway. What would that one minute and forty-five seconds have been like without Dan Hackel and the photographers, and the cutter, and the director, 'Ace' Armstrong, Bob Weisel, the assistant director, and John Davenport, the assistant producer? You know, people watch TV news shows, and they see a guy reading the news, and they think what a breeze his life is.

Figure it out for yourself here at ABC: for every man on the air, at least ten — I said *at least* — back him up. I wasn't on the air tonight, but look at me. I'm a nervous wreck. No ulcer — yet — but I deserve one."

Bruce Cohn had relaxed a little in the familiar environment of his office. Before the program he had been abrupt, his mind entirely on his one minute and forty-five seconds of air time. Now he seemed to feel like talking. So we asked him what it was that kept him in the TV spot news business. Up went his feet onto his desk, and he smiled.

"That's not so simple to put into words," said Bruce. "In a way, it's like having a front seat at a parade. For instance, I've interviewed the last four U.S. presidents, and I'm not even middle-aged! I've traveled all around the world, and my bags are packed now if I get the right assignment. I may never get home for dinner, but I'd rather have excitement than food.

"If there is one thing about TV journalism that I love, it's the *right now* quality of the work. Everything is immediate, like tonight's show; and the gratification you get, that's immediate too. You run like mad, and break your back, and when you're finished you have nothing concrete to show for it. The program goes on the air, maybe five million people watch it, and the tape goes off into the archives. It's ancient history ten minutes after it's over! But it's around. I believe that. It's around somewhere in the way people live and think! All of us in this game act on the faith that what we do makes a difference in the lives of other people, in what they do with their lives. We in TV news act on faith, I grant, but don't *you* too?"

We left Bruce Cohn sitting at his desk with his assistant producer, John Davenport, wondering aloud what tomorrow's ABC news from Washington would be like.

Disaster in the Dark

Have you ever ridden in a Krebsmobile?

Few people have—that is, besides Larry Krebs, veteran Washington TV cameraman, who prowls the district by dark, sometimes for hours on end, shooting color film for daytime news telecasts for WMAL-TV. Larry covers violence, murders and fires, follows police cars and fire trucks—wherever there is action—and stays away from diplomatic circles and the elegant night life of diplomats and high society. Larry Krebs has advice for handling the kind of society he runs into. "Carry a small bag of table salt in your pocket, and if a thug comes at you, heave it in his face. Some of it will get into his eyes and nose. Then run. Or throw a fistful of nickles at him. They will cut him up and mark him pretty well for future reference!"

Larry's advice is good—if you have to handle tough customers—and he frequently does on his late-night and early-morning beat in Washington. Larry likes to work alone, so he keeps up on all the latest and best techniques of one-man defense for his nightly rounds in the Krebsmobile.

What is the Krebsmobile?

It's a low, black, powerful General Motors late-model two-door car that puts on about 35,000 miles a year touring Washington streets. There is nothing unusual about it — except its souped-up motor and extra battery supply to operate its seven radios (four for police and fire, one an intercom with Larry Krebs' answering service and a couple of conventional FM and AM receivers). Its spacious luggage compartment contains every kind of disaster equipment imaginable — riot helmets in various colors, yellow flashing lights, fire hose, fire gear, clothing — as well as spare radio gear, a TV set, a vacuum cleaner and a general assortment of equipment designed for the safety of Larry Krebs himself and to help others in distress. It also contains a movie camera, color film, battery packs and hand-held lighting equipment. The Krebsmobile cruises like a fast tank. Its D.C. license plate is numbered 594, and it's easy to miss on a dark street when it's traveling fast.

When you ride with Larry Krebs you always make certain that your seat belt is tight, because you are never certain how fast you will go, when you will start or even where you will end up. Larry works strictly on his own; his radios, taxi drivers and policemen steer him to trouble, and, once at the scene of the action, it's up to Larry himself how much film footage for TV newscasting he's going to take and what risk it's worth. Sometimes Larry decides that it's worth his life.

A small man, light on his feet, with an explosive amount of energy, and with the complexion of a man who never sees sunlight, Krebs' sports clothes hang on him as if he has taken off a good deal of weight lately (he has). He is as bald as a grape, and he loves to talk about his twenty-five years' experience as a photograper in Washington, taking the casual visitor by surprise with his statement: "I became a photographer in the first place because my family didn't like the idea of my becoming an undertaker!" The opener is correct. Larry began his work at the age of fourteen in Bridgeport with an undertaking firm that serviced twenty-three other undertakers. "My parents were repelled with the idea that I was working with stiffs. Photography — still photography — was my road to respectability in those days."

Larry has, of course, gained considerable respectability in the years since his youth in Bridgeport, his service in the Coast Guard during World War II and his incomplete career as a college student at Yale University. Today he is a member in good standing of the White House Press Photographers' Association and has a pin to prove it. He won the association's News Photographers Award for 1966 for his TV movie coverage of a fire in 17-degree temperature on Connecticut Avenue in November of that year. He has a photograph of himself being congratulated by the President of the United States to prove it, along with the award itself. He has also gained the solid respect of his employers, WMAL-TV in Washington, as demonstrated by the enormous amount of independence and respect his employers give him.

"Larry Krebs is an authentic original," says Ted McDowell, Director of News and Public Affairs for WMAL-TV. McDowell, whose journalistic career started with the *Washington Star* in 1947, should know what he is talking about, having been with WMAL since 1952 and having majored in psychology as an undergraduate at Duke University.

"Larry first came to the station years ago. He started as

a stringer, part time, after working for International News
Photos. Washington had been his beat for years—just
about since the end of the war. There was nothing about
the district he didn't know; his contacts were unbelievable,
and his photography—black and white movie film in those
days—was great. So, about nine years ago, we hired Larry
full time. As far as I know, we're the only Washington
local TV station that has a full-time man cruising all night
and into the morning. Accordingly, we get the kind of
local film coverage they don't. In all fairness, I'll admit that
our competitors have their virtues, and sometimes they get
news stories we miss. But they don't have Larry Krebs,
and he's the ingredient that makes our news coverage distinctive.

"That's not to say that some of our first-rate producer-
directors, like Jerome Johnson, don't bring in some darn
fine documentary films for us. They do. But Larry Krebs is
distinctive. You'll find other men covering the news beats
the way he does in other cities, but only *one* per city—and
most of them not nearly as willing as Larry to risk his neck
either to bring in great film or to help out firemen, policemen or just plain citizens in distress."

While he talks about Larry a glint of envy shines in
Ted's eyes, as if he wished he were out in the street in the
Krebsmobile instead of chairbound in his spacious office,
sprinkled with reminders of his naval career and his years
with WMAL-TV. But Ted, who looks more like a college
professor than a TV executive, has his hands full running
WMAL-TV's news operation in the station's busy offices
atop a shopping center (in quarters which were previously
an ice-skating rink) at 4461 Connecticut Avenue N.W. in
Washington, D.C.

Larry himself is considerably more modest about his
career than his boss. "I just try my best," he says. "I have a

lot of friends in Washington and they help me. Then I keep my eyes open. I start work whenever I want to, eight, nine, ten or eleven o'clock at night — it doesn't matter. I have seven radios in my home, and when I don't listen to them my wife does. I stay in contact with her by radio when I go out to the garage or take a walk. Then I carry around this 'Bell Boy' gizmo." Larry removes from his pocket what looked like a small transistor radio. "This thing gives me a signal to get to a telephone or a two-way radio. I'm never very far from one or the other, and so it doesn't matter much when I start to cruise. Once I'm out, though, I'm considerably more mobile than I am at home."

Larry explains how he works. "Well," he says, "I cruise and keep my radio on and my eyes open and stop to talk with any of the twelve hundred or so Washingtonians I know personally who are out at night and might have a lead on a story. I guess I know most of the cops in town, and firemen, and night taxi drivers — to say nothing of the kids who scout for me for the fun of it. I send them all birthday cards. That's how I know there are about twelve hundred of them!"

Even when he is cruising, looking for a story, Larry does so methodically. "I cruise around DuPont Circle; that's a trouble spot. Then to 7th Street, Northwest, running up N, P, Q and on to K streets, to 4th and H. These are all principally breeding spots for trouble in Washington. Not so much crime, but fights. Then on to the bus station for a look at who's coming into town — or leaving. Then I have me a steak and french fries at 3:30 or 4:00 A.M. That's what puts the weight on!

"Then maybe I'll check Tilly's Garage. My friend Dewey Tilly runs this garage, where he keeps a batch of my radios. If Tilly thinks a story is hatching, he'll call my answering service or give it to me directly on the phone.

Then out again on my beat: downtown Washington, on the lookout for a fire, a murder or a collapsing building. Some nights, nothing happens. Some nights, I'm so busy I can't stop for a cup of tea. Why trouble comes in spurts like that I don't know, but it does!"

"I have three cardinal rules," says Larry, "and the first is that I better not take chances in getting to a story. If I have an accident, even a minor one, on my way to the action, I'll never get there, or get there late. Then I'll miss the stuff that might make good movie footage, and nobody's going to re-enact an arrest or fire for me. Second, it is my principle never to intrude in the action of firemen or policemen unless I'm asked. I try to stay out of the way of what's going on for my own safety, of course, but also not to stop the proper officials from doing their jobs effectively. And their job is not to make life easy for Larry Krebs. Last, I'm more interested in helping people in distress than in getting good movie footage. I'm sure my employers agree with me that my major obligation in the face of disaster is to be of any help to people in distress that I can be, and only second to cover the action on movie film. After all, a news show can go on the air without my pictures of a fire much more easily than a family can do without a kid, if the choice arises between helping a youngster to safety or getting good action film coverage. Anyway, what my employers think doesn't matter. They've liked me for what I am and what I do the *way* I do it, and if they don't like it, they can let me know in a very direct way with two weeks' notice. So far, they seem happy."

We arranged to meet Larry one midsummer evening at a Washington, D.C., firehouse. "That will give us a chance to have a cup of coffee with some of my friends," said Larry, meaning the firemen at the company station and a few Washington motorcycle policemen who stopped by. Larry had agreed to give us a full evening's tour in the

Krebsmobile, an honor offered few other people, he explained to us seriously. "As I told you, I'm a lone wolf," he said, "and I don't like people looking over my shoulder. But you fellows look harmless enough, and if you keep quiet and let me do my job and don't expect a guided tour, you can come along."

We swore, scouts' honor, to behave, and so we met Larry at the right time at the appointed Washington firehouse. The conversation over coffee — at 11:00 P.M. — centered on fires, disasters, fire-fighting equipment, police court and the idiosyncrasies of various traffic court judges, guessing games about how many keys Larry carries (about thirty), the virtues of law and order, and the excitement in dealing with those who violate them. The coffee was strong, and once outside the fire station Larry took a deep breath of the Washington night air. The three of us were all obviously alert and wide awake. The firehouse coffee had done its work in clearing away the cobwebs.

"Let's go!" said Larry, and we strapped ourselves into the red leather seats of the Krebsmobile. As soon as the motor started, Larry turned on each of the radio sets beneath the dashboard. Various noises started coming from the back seat. "I have the speakers located in different places so that I know which radio has which message — whether it's police, fire, my service, our station headquarters or what. In this way I don't have to recognize voices, just where the sounds come from.

"Basically, when I drive," explained Larry on the move, "I perform three operations at the same time. I drive — and that's first and most important — and second, I adjust my radios to different frequencies, and third, I listen, both to the radios and to what's going on around me. It takes a little practice, but you get used to it."

We were not used to it. The radios made a cacophony of

voices that defied interpretation, and Larry seemed to be guiding the Krebsmobile from identical street to street, continually peering out of the window on his left into the night breeze. In what seemed like a remarkably short time, we found ourselves at the District Parking Garage at 14th and I Street, on the edge of the Washington "strip." "One o'clock and no action yet," said Larry, driving into the garage. "This is Tilly's, and we can get a bite to eat at the Blue Bell Restaurant next door. I'm hungry."

While Larry downed a plate of fish and chips, we munched toast and drank more coffe. The warm night had tired us, but Larry, used to working late hours, ate energetically. "This is lunch, I guess. While you fellows were eating lunch today, I was asleep. Don't forget that! Besides, eating is my one weakness, as you can see!"

Back in the Krebsmobile, the police radio squawked something about a stolen car and an unconscious child. Larry didn't seem to be listening. Suddenly he turned up one of the speakers, and a voice said something about a fire on Wisconsin Avenue in the 1600 block. "A minor fire, he says!" said Larry. "Minor fires become major fires. Let's take a look at it."

We swerved onto a road to northwest Washington into the Georgetown district, locale of the quaint homes and clubs of the very rich as well as many of the artists and writers who live in the nation's capital. We found the fire easily enough because it was surrounded by the paraphernalia from a fire company and a remarkable number of spectators for 2:30 A.M. Larry was out of the car in an instant, light and camera in hand, looking for something to photograph. No luck!

The fire, if there had ever been one, was out, and all that was left of it was a few puffs of smoke coming through a broken window and a charred curtain, from which it had been started when a short circuit occurred in an overloaded air conditioner's electric circuit. Everything was under control except the owner of the white three-story building, a distraught lady in a bathrobe and hair curlers. The firemen, the crowd and Larry, with his lights and camera, seemed an inordinate audience for such a minor event. We felt rather silly as Larry sauntered back to the Krebsmobile, smiling.

"No pictures, no story, trifling damage," he said cheerily putting his equipment back in the trunk. "I never regret missing a fire that's been put out before it gets serious. A patrolman spotted this one and sent an alarm from a firebox. The building is just messed up a bit, but that's a problem for the owner and her insurance company. The boys had it out in three minutes. All aboard, and let's see what else we can churn up. Maybe this is a sign; trouble comes in bunches, they say."

No sooner had we reached our first intersection than Larry spotted a light-green police car, explaining that this particular automobile belonged to the United States Park Police and that he was unable to reach this particular unit's frequency on his radio. He drew up alongside the police car.

"Hello, Ed," he shouted. "Got something for me?"

The cop at the wheel shrugged, "A cute accident on the George Washington Parkway. Sort of a freak, the radio says. If you've got nothing better to do—" Larry did not wait to say "thank you!"

We were suddenly on our way to Virginia, driving now through the sticky fog which was beginning to gather in the early Washington morning. The time was 3:20. "This parkway is Federal property; that's why it comes under the jurisdiction of the Federal Government. The Park Police are responsible for it even though it's located technically in the state of Virginia. Good grief—there it is!"

Larry pulled his car onto the grass divider of the highway, and we looked out at the strange sight of a red hardtop automobile upside down, resting comfortably with one end on the ground and the other end suspended in the large trees that rimmed the roadway. As serious as it might have been, the sight looked almost ridiculous.

"What happened to the driver?" asked Larry of the first policeman he found after parking.

The officer smiled. "Saved by a seat belt, Larry! Just shaken up and a couple of cuts on his forehead. He's sitting in my car now, kinda dazed. Says he doesn't want an ambulance. He may get a good rest out of all of this, though. We found papers in the car revoking his driver's license; he says the car isn't paid for, and he may be drunk. We'll find out for certain when we get to the station."

A tow truck pulled up to the scene, which had gathered an eerie collection of police cars, with their whirling red-and-white lights, along with the truck sending yellow beacons into the sky. The traffic was backed up into the foggy gloom as far as we could see. The tow truck driver was attaching the hook at the end of his winch onto the bumper of the car.

Larry ran to his luggage compartment. "Turning the car over is going to be interesting. I'll get it on film." Larry went into action as the winch first pulled the car perpendicular to the roadway and then let it down with a noisy crunch onto the roadbed. The driver, tears running down his face, had left the police car and looked at the twisted mess of what had once been a proud red roadster. He seemed to want to apologize to someone, but nobody paid any attention to him. Now the police began letting traffic pass the spot of the accident.

"Nothing else for us here," said Larry Krebs as we slipped into his black automobile. In no time at all we found ourselves back in Washington, outside Tilly's Garage, where we enjoyed steaming coffee in paper containers while sitting on the fence of a construction site. At exactly 4:25 A.M., Larry heard something on his car radio and motioned to us to join him.

"Get in fellows. This is it! A railroad station is burning down!" The Krebsmobile was on its way, joined now by a police car, now by a jeep with fire-fighting equipment, now by a fire officer's automobile. As we sped to northeast Washington, down Sherman Avenue to New Hampshire Avenue and Blair Road on the Maryland border, Larry gathered a small team of official automobiles around his car which gave him sanction to pass through red lights and stop signs. The racket of sirens from the accompanying vehicles was nerve-shattering. Larry was talking, but we couldn't hear him.

Suddenly we saw it! Flames reached up into the sky from a two-story wooden structure that was clearly outlined against the near-purple sky. We halted in a little valley that might once have been a parking lot near the station. As Larry put on his fire boots, coat, helmet and battery pack, he told us about the flaming depot. "That is the old Tacoma Park Railroad Station. It dates back one-hundred years, I guess. Folks say that President Lincoln's funeral train made its first stop here. As far as I know, the station house hasn't been used for anything but storage for years, although Baltimore and Ohio trains use the tracks and commuter trains still stop here. The building is a genuine antique — a dry antique, as you can see — and I guess it will burn like a matchbox. If we're lucky, nobody will be hurt and we'll get some magnificent fire pictures."

With Larry in the lead, we scrambled up a metal staircase to the station, now an inferno, with five firehoses playing on it and dozens of firemen hard at their individual jobs. Heavy gray smoke rose from the structure, and the spray from the hoses and steam of the fire made the atmosphere as thick, sooty and foggy as a swamp on a summer afternoon. Larry, in his fireman's gear, had disappeared among the other fire coats and helmets.

We were standing in two inches of water, the spray from the firehoses playing on our jackets and trousers. We had no questions now about why Larry wore a fire coat: for protection against flames, and to keep dry! We looked around and noted that we were the only onlookers who were not wearing protective clothing.

Larry was at our side again. "A two-alarm fire!" he exclaimed. "You can say it's a two-alarm fire — which means roughly that four fire-fighting units are involved. There must be 100 firemen here — and take a look at all that equipment packed below that ledge there!" We saw an army of trucks and piles of hoses being rushed up from the parking area to the station. "They must be using 35 pieces of equipment, at least. See that fireman up there?"

We looked around and saw a young fireman, who appeared to have stepped out of a recruiting poster, playing a gigantic hose on the roof of the structure. "What a picture!" said Larry. He held up his camera to photograph the fireman, his slick coat shining in the reflection of the flames and Larry's lights. The fireman saw Larry, smiled and waved. "Great!" said Larry. "Now I want to get some footage from the other side of the station. Coming?"

Without listening to our apology — that we felt happier, and safer, where we were — Larry was off to get more pictures. Now the fire and the pressure of water had exposed the skeleton of the building's framework through its upper dormers. "I think she's under control," said a tall fireman near us, running off to help a team break into a locked door. The time was 5:00 A.M. by now, without a sign of the Washington sunrise in the sky. The thick smoke around us would have been insufferable had not a little breeze begun to clear the air. We were drenched to the skin.

Larry came running up to us. "I want to get some footage of that roof if she caves in. Thank heavens, no one was hurt," he observed as he placed his camera down on the tailgate of a fire truck and began to reload his camera. "The trick," he said, "in changing film under conditions like this is not to look down at the camera and pour a bucket of water from your helmet into the instrument. Here, hold this light, please!" Larry reached for a new reel from his pocket and began to replace the old one. "Drat," he said, "I got the shutter wet!" After a few more minutes of fiddling, the camera was loaded. He held it up. "Let's see if I can get anything else. The fire is out, for all practical purposes. Firemen will keep at it, though, for the next seven or eight hours, putting out embers here and there and smothering potential trouble spots."

We waited for Larry to return. "I call it a night!" he said, sopping in his fire coat, water dripping from the rim of his fire hat and his boots caked with mud. "What about you?" We said it was a night indeed, and we followed him back to the Krebsmobile, where we all used his towels and he packed away his gear into its proper places.

On the road again, Larry was feeling expansive. The action had keyed him up. "You won't see a fire like that every day. No sir! I guess you fellows got what you were looking for!" We agreed.

"You were lucky," said Larry. "The B&O Railroad wasn't, but you were. You can't ever predict where the action will come from or when. The footage I've taken — if everything goes right and it was exposed properly, *and* if it isn't ruined in processing — will be on tomorrow's late-afternoon TV news shows. And notice one thing:

WMAL-TV is the only local station that covered this action with film. The others will use stills, and the newspaper photographers won't even get to her until daylight."

Larry's words reminded us to look outside and notice that the sun was rising on a sleepy Washington. It was well after 6:00 A.M. Larry put some music on the radio. "Can I drop you at your hotel? Then I have to get my film back to the station."

We thanked Larry Krebs for his graciousness and for the privilege of joining him in the Krebsmobile and, once inside our hotel rooms, peeled off our drenched clothes, bathed and collapsed into exhausted sleep.

While we were sleeping, the morning newspapers were put under our doors. All the Washington journals covered the story of the Tacoma Railroad Station fire. It made the front page of one. *The Washington Post*, for instance, ran two daylight photographs (Larry was right) of the skeletal building with the following story:

"The Tacoma Park Railroad Station in Northeast Washington, built just before the turn of the century [the other papers repeated the Lincoln funeral legend], was gutted yesterday by a fire that may have been set by vandals. . . . The Baltimore and Ohio Railroad discontinued using the station ten years ago, but trains have been stopping to pick up Washington commuters from its platform."

We could hardly wait to see the TV color coverage later in the afternoon and the on-the-spot photography made by the remarkable Larry Krebs himself.

8

TV Eyes the Nation

When they built 30 Rockefeller Plaza, the home office of the NBC network, in the 1930s, nobody was concerned with TV news coverage. Nobody had even heard of it!

The building, smack in the center of what was once called Radio City, faces the world-renowned Rockefeller Plaza, with its wintertime skating rink, famous imported Christmas tree and tulip festival in the spring. To the west, it stands on New York's Sixth Avenue (officially The Avenue of the Americas). Deep in the basement of "Thirty Rock," as it is affectionately known, you'll find subway entrances, a post office, stores of every description and a variety of eating places.

Thirty Rock was built originally as a home for the Radio Corporation of America, NBC's parent organization, and since its opening the side entrances have announced that the "NBC Studios" were located inside. In the 1930s, the studios were devoted, of course, entirely to radio broadcasting. (Somewhere, in those days, inventors in the

RCA laboratories were tinkering with a new-fangled gadget called "television." Sightseers who took a guided tour of the slick, modern NBC radio studios were given a brief demonstration of how TV would someday work and had a chance to look at their friends on a tiny twelve-inch TV screen.)

Since the thirties, almost every inch of Thirty Rock has been remodeled, rebuilt and reoccupied many times. What was once America's largest radio operation (made up of two prosperous networks at its height) now houses NBC radio and TV operations, as well as the offices, studios and facilities of the network-owned and -operated New York stations. RCA, the parent company, still dominates the building, in which various office spaces for all kinds of enterprises are located. The familiar banks of elevators to the "NBC Studios," manned by clean-cut, uniformed operators, continue to attract the tourists, waiting to watch the taping of a TV show, passing through on endless guided tours or just gawking to catch the sight of a celebrity on his way to or from a broadcast, a rehearsal or an interview.

NBC's newsroom on the fifth floor looks as if it had seen many, many changes in its time. It has. Once you get past the front facade of promotional displays and the fishbowl radio studios, where broadcasters and engineers carry out their activities behind soundproof glass windows, you walk into what looks like a giant city room of a newspaper that never gets printed. TV sets in black and white and color are set into overhead fixtures, but nobody seems to have set their volume levels very high. Writers and editors pore over the endless miles of ticker tape that news services provide, speak quietly into a multitude of telephones and live in an atmosphere which, twenty-four hours a day, can best be described as one of "controlled tension." There is nothing slick or modern about the NBC newsroom; the entire area has been designed with an eye to utility alone, and no one seems to care how many coffee containers litter a typewriter table or whether someone likes to keep his feet on the desk while he reads a press report.

Most (probably at least two-thirds) of the people who work in the newsroom never see the lens of a live TV camera. According to Rex Goad, NBC's Director of News, the vast majority of the more than one hundred people, employed in the newsroom and its allied operations, remain relatively anonymous, never wear TV make-up and never go on the air. They represent the enormous backstop team standing behind and next to every on-the-spot TV reporter we see on our home receivers.

Wander around the newsroom long enough and you'll find the offices of Don Meaney, Vice-President of NBC News, a veteran newsman in his late forties who earned his gray hairs in the radio-TV spot reporting business. After his graduation from Rutgers University's School of Journalism, Don went to work at a nearby New Brunswick, New Jersey, radio station in 1947 for the grand sum of $35 per week. Four or five years later, he moved over to NBC and has been there ever since — "moving up the ladder," in his own words. Organization and logistics are his main job: tasks like following Nikita Khrushchev on his visit to America in 1959, keeping up with the Presidents and figuring out how to cover political conventions with a minimum of confusion and disorder.

Don's job is to head up NBC-TV's national on-the-spot coverage — live coverage wherever possible: how to get men and equipment to the scene of the action while a news story is breaking or, more often, *after* it has broken and how to make this kind of TV coverage, which is now in color, both accurate and visually interesting.

Don is still excited, justifiably, about the problems NBC

encountered in covering the Glassboro, New Jersey, meeting between Soviet Premier Aleksei Kosygin and President Johnson in late June of 1967. Don says that he never had to solve so many news problems in so short a time to get this historic conference onto NBC's TV screens. Nor has he ever been so frustrated by what he could not accomplish. But let him tell about it in his own words:

"One of the greatest tests in national coverage that NBC-TV has had in recent years was that summit conference. This occurred on extremely short notice. Of course, there had been rumors that Johnson and Kosygin would get together, but we had nothing concrete to plan on. We thought, obviously, that they would meet in Washington, New York or some normal place like Camp David. And, more obviously, no one thought of Glassboro, New Jersey — or had even heard of Glassboro.

"I don't recall exactly how much time we had; I think it was less than twenty-four hours! We heard early one Thursday evening that they were going to meet the next day at Glassboro! We needed an immediate mobilization of equipment and men. At least, everybody was alert to the fact that something might happen, so we knew where all the equipment was — where the bodies were, so to speak. We were staying what we call 'a little loose' just in the event of a meeting coming up.

"We immediately organized a large body of all kinds of people: engineers and technicians, of course, but also news managers and correspondents and people who could 'run' things at the scene, all brought from Washington and New York. We drew in equipment from our own supplies here in New York and Washington too, and also from our affiliated station in Philadelphia. We got a mobile unit from them.

"The difficulty was tremendous in an operation like this, because nobody who was running the show knew exactly what he was doing. Once we got the mobile units and the people on the way, even on the scene, we didn't know what to do with them! No one knew *how* Johnson would arrive, for example, so where should a camera be placed for his arrival? Nor did we know how Kosygin was going to arrive—he came by car—so we had to guess again.

"In all of these events where you don't know what to expect or coverage is physically limited, the three networks immediately pool their resources. While we prize our competition, one with the other, and defend it at every opportunity, there are times when we recognize that sometimes we just can't go it alone. Our aim is to get the best coverage possible on our network. In this case, as usual, pooling created difficulties because each network wanted what it considered the best vantage point to cover the event for its own cameras and correspondents.

"The result was that the organizational problem was eased but also heightened by the pool operation. Gradually, we found out what was going to happen. But it was the worst spot broadcasting problem we had ever confronted. We never did get on the air properly that Friday. We had pictures coming up here to New York completely unidentified as to network and entirely confusing in content. We got into internetwork arguments concerning what was a pool picture and what wasn't, and who could use what when. Here in New York the news executives were on the phone with each other, demanding and refusing live pictures and making more chaos.

"The biggest problem was the New Jersey Bell Telephone Company. The demand on them for lines was just as short, immediate, urgent and desperate as it was on us! They just weren't able to rise to it; they had never really been involved in this kind of TV activity before. Our coverage was awful, and the telephone company was little help in getting pictures from Glassboro to New York.

"We had two days' grace before the next summit meeting the following Sunday, and by then everything was in good order. We had a classic pickup. Everything worked and everybody was in the right place, and the phone company was on the ball.

"Associated with TV coverage, however, is the problem of *what you do* with your material *after* you cover it. Our decision was immediate and automatic. We decided to cover, live, every possible event that could be shown at Glassboro and concerning the summit. Our plan was to start out covering Kosygin when he left the Russian Consulate on Park Avenue in New York, which we did. We tried to cover President Johnson's departure from the White House in the same way and again at Philadelphia airport, where his jet plane delivered him. Then we showed him taking a helicopter to Glassboro and the landing.

"We stayed on the air all the time the two men were in the building—which requires a lot of 'backing and filling' by the staff on the air, but it's our experience that once you get with a story like this, if you want to hold the audience, you just stay on the air with it. The people who are interested are not going to wait for you if you go off the air and back to regular programming. You never know when someone is going to pop out of a door and make an announcement, so we covered it from front to back. By the time Sunday night rolled around—and we had been doing this sort of coverage all day Sunday as well—a difficult problem arose because of Kosygin's suddenly announced press conference at the United Nations.

"We were committed to ourselves to cover it, and it required a complete shift of our Sunday-night programming. We dropped certain programs and kept others.

These decisions required a tremendous amount of telephoning, especially on a Sunday night, with everybody at
home. The whole problem was discussed with the programming department, the head of NBC news and even
the head of NBC, just to try to figure out how best to serve
both the network's and the public's interests before and
after the event. The Glassboro meeting and its aftermath
were classical combinations of confusion and difficulties! I
can't begin to think of any event that caused us so many
and such severe problems."

Bill Corrigan, Director of Operations for NBC News,
had been listening to Don's laments about the Glassboro
summit meeting. Bill, a native of Connecticut who has had
twenty years' experience at both NBC and CBS, added his
own recollections of that weekend in June.

"Don is absolutely correct," says Bill. "Everything at
Glassboro had to be done live or at least on tape. The
event was too big—too important—to wait for film to be
processed, and it was too big not to cover any part of it
that we possibly could—as it happened. Well, our first
problem that Thursday night was to find out where in
heaven's name Glassboro was! Then the logistics problems
came up, just as Don said. How do you get a TV signal
from a place that was totally unprepared? It was quite a
mess.

"Friday we got on the air, but the picture looked like an
early silent movie, edited by an ape, mostly because of our
utter dependency upon the telephone company to transmit
the TV image, which they only partially succeeded in
doing. They tried, but for some reason they also thought
they had an obligation to carry regular phone calls as well
as service the TV networks! By Sunday, of course, we had
straightened things out with them, and we could beef up
and increase our own operations on the spot.

"In both instances we were doing live broadcasting and

taping, but we were also filming. We had a great gaggle of people on the event, so, one way or another, we caught all the news there was to catch, I'd say. Certainly, more than one hundred NBC people were involved, one way or another, all the way from engineers to copy boys, from correspondents, sound men, radio engineers, legmen, deskmen, editors, couriers, and supervisors for the works — even a Citizens Band radio unit to communicate by walkie-talkies to all personnel involved. We had airplanes and helicopters involved in it to fly over the Jersey turnpike to follow Kosygin's car and to fly a crew to a little island off the Jersey coast because Kosygin's daughter was visiting there!

"Don't ask me — or Don — how much it cost NBC to cover the Glassboro conference. We don't know, and we wouldn't want to guess! I try not to think about things like that. Pool operations give us enough trouble without worrying too hard or long how much they cost."

Don Meaney nodded. "We can't waste money, but we can't afford not to cover an event like Glassboro simply because of what it costs. You move to obtain the coverage and worry about the bills later. And we don't save money often by pooling facilities with the other networks either. All we do is expand our own coverage in a pool, but we still have plenty of individual work to do as a network operation in a pooled broadcast, all of which is pretty expensive and usually elaborate as well.

"A good example is the space shots from Cape Kennedy. The principal shots at Cape Kennedy are pooled: the 'lift-off,' certain locations where special equipment like the giant camera we used down there (which is the only one in the world), and locations where there is room for only one camera, such as the spot where the astronauts board the elevator and go up to the spacecraft. There are also NASA 'official' cameras, some of them close-up cameras, from towers and restricted places which every network uses, because they can't cover these scenes themselves. Then there is the pool's own set of cameras, which are spotted around for the 'lift-off' itself to cover it from every possible angle.

"In addition, each network has its own anchor position, where Dave Brinkley, in our case, or Cronkite, in CBS's case, sits on camera in such a manner that you can show both the man and the pool picture off in the background. Beyond that, there are the studio embellishments that must be added to the coverage, because there is so darn little to show during a space flight after the capsule lifts off. But you want to stay on the air and keep the public up to date. When the flights go on for days on end, of course, we don't stay on the air all the time. But when something important happens, each network is then on its own to decide whether to cover it or not.

"We here at NBC have a giant studio in this building — 8H to be exact — which is just filled with graphic material to illustrate how and what the spacemen are doing. For example, we have a full-sized, completely accurate scale spacecraft of our own! We *build* a Gemini or Apollo space capsule model for demonstration purposes. We use miniature spacecraft and rockets (which don't look undersized on camera) showing the maneuvering, how they join one another and that kind of operation in space. For space walks, we elected to use hand puppets, made by the Bairds, which show how the men get out of their craft and pull the lines and take their pictures and so forth. We also use giant maps which show the progress of the astronauts across the world and all kinds of other visual aids. This is the way that we at NBC *individualize* what is basically a pooled TV story. If possible, we never want to use pooled materials without giving them a distinctive NBC slant of some kind.

"Even at Glassboro, our Friday coverage, though poor, was distinctively our own, and we take both credit and responsibility for its virtues and its faults. We'll accept as much credit as you want to give us for the Sunday coverage and for the way tape and film clips were prepared and fed to our five owned and operated stations, as well as to our affiliated TV stations around the country. They depend largely upon NBC network or NBC's News Syndication Service for national news coverage. The service, incidentally, was started in 1961. It provides wider news coverage over closed circuit TV to our affiliates than our regular news programs. It also covers more subjects, like sports, in which our affiliates are interested."

Don Meaney paused for a moment. "NBC," he said, "is the oldest network still on the air. True, it started out in radio and is no older than the others as a TV medium. But it still has its traditions, which go back to the beginnings of broadcasting. Here on the fifth floor of Thirty Rock it's our business to see that NBC news keeps up that tradition — that wherever the news breaks in the United States or anywhere, we cover it, or at least bust our backs in the attempt. I'm just one man out of some 100 people here whose job it is to make sure that NBC will be on the spot at the *next* Glassboro conference, *wherever* in the world it may be held — and however many headaches it may give us!"

9

Warfare in the Streets

This is the story that Lem Tucker told us about the riots in the Negro districts of Newark, New Jersey, East Harlem, New York, and Bedford-Stuyvesant in Brooklyn during the summer of 1967. It's not a happy story.

Lem Tucker is an NBC-TV reporter who saw the riots first hand. He was shot at by snipers, had bottles and Molotov cocktails hurled in his direction and wore a soldier's "tin helmet" to protect his head from flying objects. You may well have seen Lem's TV films on your home set if you watched TV at all that blood-soaked summer.

Lem is twenty-nine years old, a graduate of Central Michigan University, a veteran of the Army who served in Vietnam. He started working at NBC as a page, moving on to editorial jobs and finally to his present position as a reporter. He is an efficient, confident newsman, and he is confident that he has a profitable future in TV. He hates covering race riots.

He should. Lem Tucker is a Negro. The riots in the

streets during the summer of 1967 have left a particularly bitter taste in his mouth. He speaks of them quietly—almost objectively. His training as a reporter has taught him to control his emotions and "get the story across" despite any personal feelings.

We met Lem on the fifth floor of the NBC studios, and he told us about his experiences as we followed him on a daily routine assignment. This is how the riots of 1967 looked to him, and these are his words, exactly as we heard them:

"Let's see. I was made an NBC reporter just a week before the Newark riots. They started on Thursday, July 13. No! For all practical purposes that was the second night of the action. But this was the *big* night. I was a reporter in charge of a three-man crew—four people, including myself: a cameraman, a sound man and a light technician. We were there together to get film footage of the action—to shoot what was going on. This was what I did, beginning on that Thursday, and I went on through until about 9:00 P.M. the following Sunday, when I was pulled out of Newark and sent to New Brunswick and to Plainfield, New Jersey, where some protests were starting. Then I was in East Harlem and Brooklyn, but the big one I covered was in Newark. It was a terrible experience.

"Nothing much happened the first night. We were marooned in front of the police station with policemen telling how it was unsafe for us. And, of course, every time we stuck our noses beyond the policed area we found out it was unsafe. Among other things, I was under gunfire in Newark for the first time in my life. You see, in Vietnam I had an administrative post in Saigon, but in the streets of Newark I ended up under sniper fire, right in the middle of a police gun duel with a sniper.

"I wasn't looking for trouble or running unnecessary

risks. That would have been stupid, although just being there might have been stupid, depending on how you look at it. We drove into some areas where there were no police, where there was minor action to photograph, where we knew that we'd have to depend on our own ingenuity and the speed of our car to get out — when and if we were caught in sniper fire.

"Frankly, to *be* in Newark at that time was a risk, and to be with a TV crew was more of a risk, even on a street that the police had called 'safe' the day before. You never knew where gunfire would start. We ran a risk with police as well as with rioters, because sometimes, as we approached, they couldn't recognize us. We covered the story in unmarked cars, naturally, because TV reporters were not exactly popular with the crowd.

"I don't think we caused any problems — although, you know, it has been charged that TV reporters and cameras and crews would sometimes stir up a crowd to riot. Nothing like this happened in *my* experiences. Neither my crew nor I caused any action, I'm sure of that. Things were well under way before we got there.

"I learned a lot in Newark. I learned an awful lot — not just as a reporter but as a Negro and as a man. I'll admit — not too proudly — that I've led something of a sheltered life. I have never experienced many of the bitter things that American Negroes have lived through in our country today. I guess I've been lucky, but I just can't claim that I've ever been the victim of real discrimination! Not somebody who has my job at my age! Actually, an awareness of racial discrimination came to me later in my life than I'm proud of admitting. I learned an awful lot in the streets of Newark.

"I suppose it was nothing I didn't know, but I saw evidence of it. I heard and saw people who I hadn't been around in a ghetto like the Newark colored district for years. I was back there — with them. I knew what they were talking about, angry about. I remembered — as I heard some of these people rant and rave and curse — what things are like in a ghetto. I suppose — with some of the breaks I've had — I've forgotten. I seriously wondered — as a human being *and* a Negro — if I had been pulling my fair share. I decided that I probably hadn't, that I needed to be more involved in the problems of urban ghettos like the ones in Newark and Harlem. I'd gotten back to some things I needed to know. It brought home the fact that things are still pretty bad in these districts — in the same places that they've been pretty bad for too long. I knew why these people were out there — *why* they were rioting.

"What do you go after for TV coverage in a situation like Newark? Well, that's difficult to say. You want to go for the action; you want to show what's happening. At the same time, you don't want to distort it and make it look worse than it is — or better. But there are other stories which, unfortunately, you cannot show at the time when you are actually there on the spot. There's so much you see that you want to cover! Sometimes you can get a human-interest shot, or interview people afterwards — children, old ladies — or you have to go back the next day to cover the heart of the story, or wait until the action subsides.

"We go where the action is! We have to. In Newark, I was concerned about my own safety and the safety of the crew I was with, but there are times you are forced to take risks. When I got to East Harlem, for instance, I found that I drew a blank as to what to be afraid of, or what fear was. Maybe it was because I was green as a reporter, or maybe I was just tired, but I thought primarily about getting the story.

"In all the riots, of course, we didn't ask for trouble.

Whenever possible, we avoided going into areas where there were no police around. We tried to keep our equipment and lights out of sight when there was no action going on. When people criticize TV reporters in spots like these and say we stir up trouble, they don't realize that we're just as interested in keeping out of the way for our own safety as we are in getting a TV film story!

"Did I find myself editorializing or slanting my news stories because of my prejudices as a Negro? That's quite a question! No — or, at least, I hope not. That's tough to answer, because here I was, a Negro covering Negro riots, and I'm sure that my employers and the TV audience were looking for some slanting on my part. If I *did* show any sign of partiality, I was sure someone would catch it. I'd say that I probably leaned over backwards to avoid grinding an ax or propagandizing. I tried to give a straight, factual account of what went on, when it happened, the visible results and the most objective account I could. It's difficult — don't misunderstand — it's difficult to look at something as tragic as the Newark riots and not be stirred. It's especially difficult for a Negro, I think.

"The biggest frustration I felt, I suppose, was that it was still there, the urban ghetto, the segregated neighborhood, the poverty. I asked myself what my responsibility was? You can only tell a part of the story at any one time. I kept wanting to tell *more*. I kept wanting to tell it *all*. I wanted to get a deeper look, a deeper study — not just of what's happening here during the summer of 1967 — but *why* it keeps happening to these people every season for years and years. But remember, this was my *first* story, except for one other day of city reporting, and so there was a personal involvement and an unbelievable desire to do a good job and satisfy my superiors at NBC.

"Sometimes I wondered, 'What am I doing here? Why

am I walking down a street where a sniper may take a pot shot at me?' People were throwing bottles and rocks at police and garbage into the streets and sometimes these missiles at newsmen — and I kept thinking that I spent all those months in Vietnam to come home to the U.S. to take a bullet, maybe, or a brick to my head in Newark, New Jersey. I think my most recurrent thought through the entire experience was that I'd been to a war zone for eleven months and felt much safer there than I did on the streets of America during the riots!

"Riots? Call them rebellions, insurrections, demonstrations, protests — call them anything you want! To my way of thinking, East Harlem and Bedford-Stuyvesant were *not* riots, even by the simplest definition. Newark *was* a riot — once it was out there in the streets, wrecking police stations and looting and burning and shooting. Bombs were dropping. It was unbelievable. You had to be in it to understand. One small incident started it, but panic spread like brush fire. Everybody was frightened — the police, the national guard. This was warfare in the streets, but nobody knew who the enemy was!"

Lem told us his story in bits and pieces, in between a trip in an NBC car through Central Park and on to an assignment that took him uptown in New York City. We traveled with a three-man camera crew.

At his destination, Lem looked troubled. He obviously had more to say about the riots of 1967, but he had work to do. Could we meet him tomorrow at his office? We could and did.

The next day Lem had changed his dark suit and knitted tie for sports clothes — the latest in a turtleneck shirt and loafers. It was his day off, but he looked troubled rather than relaxed when we met him. We guessed that he had not talked himself out on the subject of the riots, and we were correct. He had been doing some thinking about them—disturbed thinking—which he wanted us to hear. It was relatively quiet in the NBC newsroom.

"I was thinking, first of all, that maybe you'd be interested in how it was, working with an integrated crew—a white crew, that is—from my point of view. We do a lot of joking about integration, but it isn't always a joke. It wasn't in Newark, where I had to tell people that the crew was with *me* for their safety. But we all learn from situations like this.

"I don't think a Negro crew would have done any better than integrated crews did in Newark. I don't believe in playing games. For instance, there were meetings held by Black Power people where no white pressmen were admitted—only the Negro press. I think we—meaning NBC—should always boycott them, plain and simple. I don't think people have any right to select the reporters who will cover their meetings. But I don't think you can write the Black Power people off, although I don't think the press should yield to their demands either.

"For instance, on Friday, July 21, a Black Power conference was held in Newark, and hostility mounted towards the press. The leaders didn't want us there—black or white, but especially white. By Saturday afternoon, the antagonism had risen to the degree that the most militant Black Power group had taken control of the meeting. During a press conference, Saturday afternoon, a disturbance in the hall caused us all to turn our heads in that direction. And a couple of seconds later the leaders came storming in screaming, 'Let's get 'em; let's get 'em out of here, ' meaning the white press. The result was sheer pandemonium! People were everywhere, jumping out of windows, out of doors. They overturned cameras and damaged equipment. It was planned: a show of force!

"This fracas was designed to demonstrate to the moderate Black Power people *and* the press that the radicals were in control. Some people are still trying to live down this particular incident that was covered on live TV tape and got wide distribution.

"One interesting thing: somebody said to me afterwards — a Negro fellow — 'You better get out of here. Remember, the white press here, they're just dirty liars,' he said. 'But *you*, you're a traitor *and* a dirty liar.' He made it very clear that this is the way the real militants feel about the press, black or white. They feel that Negroes like me have sold out, no matter how we cover race problems. They say we're working for what they call the W.P.P., the White Power Press. Interestingly enough, NBC had three Negroes — Bill Matney, Greg Harris and me — working on the Newark riots. None of us has sold out to anybody, I'd say, but some Negroes don't look at the problem the way we do.

"Not that this criticism shook me. I've been called a traitor by some part of the black community all my life, and I'm used to it. Maybe too used to it. It always rolled off more than it should have, maybe. I don't feel that I've been a traitor. I just feel I've gotten too far away from the realities of Negro life in America. That's easy to do in Rockefeller Center!

"How do I feel about the W.P.P.? I don't feel anything. NBC has asked just one thing of me since I've been reporting for them, and that is that I do my best job, a *factual* job. I'm not here to editorialize. That isn't my business, and I've never been asked to color a story — pardon the word — one way or another, regardless of what it has been about!

"One thing the Negroes who are so abusive of the White Power Press forget is the key contribution that TV and other news media have made in bringing about social progress and better conditions for the Negroes by calling attention, over the years, to the way they've been treated in many parts of the United States—and the need for change and legislation for equal rights. The picture, remember, of dogs being turned on Negroes in Alabama did more to get a Civil Rights Bill through Congress than all the pious preaching of black and white liberals for a hundred years! It's tragically ironic that so many Black Power people fault the press for being unfair to Negroes when the broadcasting news people, especially, have done so much to dramatize segregation today in the U.S.A.

"As far as the riots are concerned, I'm convinced that last summer's, at least, began spontaneously. The Black Power people of any degree of militancy can't and don't gather together all the tiny understandable causes that spark one outburst—like Newark. On the other hand, I'm aware of the fact that there are those individuals sitting around who have plans to exploit these incidents once they begin. I'm not surprised by this one bit. Gosh, there have been, of course, people who move into events like these to their own profit all through history. Self-interest among Negroes is as powerful a motive as it is among any other group, and some of it is, in my opinion, harmful self-interest. Anyone who exploits violence is asking for trouble.

"I guess I ought to say a word or two about myself—as a reporter and as a Negro. When I came back from Vietnam, I didn't come back saying, 'I want to be a reporter.' So I'm surprised that I got to the position I'm in here at NBC for a couple of reasons. First, I've had some breaks without having had certain experiences—say, a stint as a reporter for a newspaper or wire service—because people had faith in me and took a chance. Second, I can't hedge the fact that I have found certain benefits—that I've tried desperately not to take advantage of—of being a Negro. But there's also an additional burden if you're put together like I am, because you try that much harder and look at yourself and realize how much you have to learn. I'm still wet behind the ears! I need plenty of hard work and experience to succeed in this profession, and perhaps someday see it from the side of management, where I might be able to play a role in the growth of TV news."

Lem had had his say. The disturbed look had passed from his features, and his mood changed.

"One more thing," he said. "The TV audience is rarely aware of what reporters and crews have to go through to cover the news. Cameras, sound equipment and lights are heavy and tough to carry, all the worse in a midsummer riot. TV coverage doesn't just happen! Most people don't realize that the nuts and bolts of this business are complicated and exhausting."

Lem added vehemently, "I hate riots. I've heard people say — in the heat of a situation like Newark — 'Boy, the TV guys love this!' No, we don't! Not a bit, and especially not me! I hope I never cover another riot in my life — and this includes riots by anyone because of anything. And I'd just as soon run out of wars to cover as soon as possible.

"Violence is hell. But once it starts, our business is covering it on TV, so that the people will know what's going on. True, a great part of the public *has* been critical of TV lately and the way we handled situations like Newark. But if those riots had happened, and the public *had not seen one bit of film or tape*, these same people would have accused us of trying to *cover it up* for any number of reasons. In this business, I'm sure you've seen the continual effort — which is necessary — to make sure that we all take seriously our responsibilities to cover the news honestly. I think we've been doing a good job — but I also know darn well we can do better if we want to."

10

How TV Covers the Globe

CBS corporate headquarters are housed in a super-modern skyscraper on 52nd Street in New York City. *Life* magazine ran a picture story on the interior decorations of the building. It is an architectural marvel, served by computer-run elevators and an automated system of mail delivery. "Pop" art objects adorn the walls of the cafeteria, and a resident gardener keeps the office foliage green and well trimmed. The bright young men and the pretty secretaries also look well cared for, well trimmed and proud of "their" skyscraper.

If you are ever in New York, drop in to 51 West 52nd Street! Say we sent you, and they will treat you as courteously as anyone else.

But keep away from the CBS Production Studios!

They are — or were — literally a barn. A cow barn: one of the last kept within the city limits of Manhattan, where a milk company once provided whole fresh milk at premium prices for ailing or finicky city dwellers.

What makes it, in fact, an ideal production center for CBS is space, pure and simple. Located near the Hudson River on New York's midtown west side, it fills nearly half a block of this relatively low-rent district with networks of corridors, studios, offices, projection theaters, technical facilities and other installations that need room to operate and spread out. Wandering around the corridors of the CBS Production Studios is good training for working in the Pentagon. And its voluminous interior, its magnificent loading dock (where once milk carts were filled for their daily round) and its location in the midst of numerous parking garages make it an ideal spot for the nerve center of the world-wide CBS-TV production operation.

Just don't get lost in it, or it is likely to take you all day to get out!

When you start talking at the CBS Production Studios about overseas coverage, eventually the names of Bob Little and Marshall Davidson come up in conversation. You never see those names on your TV tube — at least, not long enough to read them — and neither man claims to be a frustrated newscaster. They both work together as closely as identical twins, and sometimes, when you are talking to them, Bob starts a sentence and Marshall finishes it. Even when they disagree, they nod at each other.

Robert A. Little is, officially, Foreign Assignment Editor of CBS, and Marshall B. Davidson is Director of Film Services. Bob is a scholarly, soft-spoken man of about forty; Marshall talks like a slightly muted bull-horn with a New England accent and is a hefty extrovert about six years older. Their jobs dovetail in so many ways, so many times, as to demand identical responsibilities from both of them; hence the pseudo-partnership.

"CBS covers the world," says Bob. "Let's see. We have bureaus in Mexico City, Tokyo, Hong Kong, Bangkok,

Walter Cronkite, *CBS News*

William Lawrence, *ABC News*, Political Correspondent, Washington, on White House lawn

Elmer W. Lower, President,
ABC News

Richard S. Salant, President,
CBS News

William R. McAndrew, President,
NBC News
died while book was on press

Donald Meaney, Vice President,
NBC News

Lem Tucker, Reporter, *NBC News*

Ev Aspinwald, Manager TV News,
ABC News, Washington

William Corrigan, Director of
Operations, *NBC News*

Rex Goad, Director of News, *NBC News*

Charles Collingwood, Chief
Foreign Correspondent, *CBS News*,
in Vietnam

Marshall Davidson, Director
of Film Services, *CBS News*

Don Hackel, *ABC* White House
Reporter

Robert Little, Foreign Assignment
Editor, *CBS News*

Mike Wallace, *CBS News* Correspondent, interviews captured Egyptian generals at a POW camp in Israel

Richard C. Hottelet, *CBS* U. N. Correspondent (left) interviewing Silvert Andreas Nielsen, former President of Security Council

NBC GLOBAL WEATHER

GEMINI CONTROL

MINS. SECS.

Chet Huntley and David Brinkley, *NBC News*, during the Gemini space shot

Robin Still, *CBS* Cameraman, ready for a jump with the Air Force

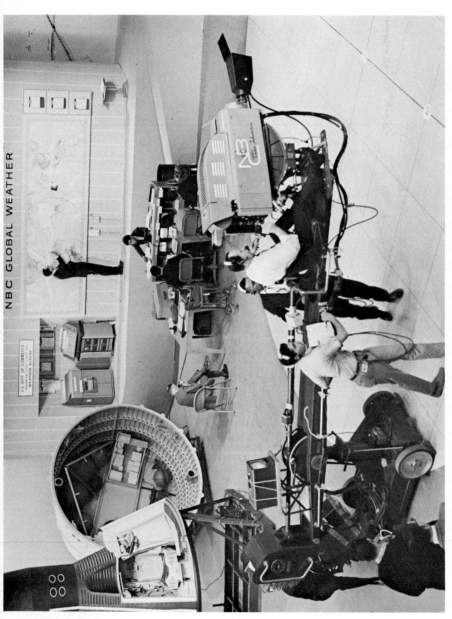

Dr. Frank Field, *NBC* Meteorologist, during Gemini space shot. Exact model of capsule at left

Frank McGee, *NBC News* Correspondent during Gemini space shot

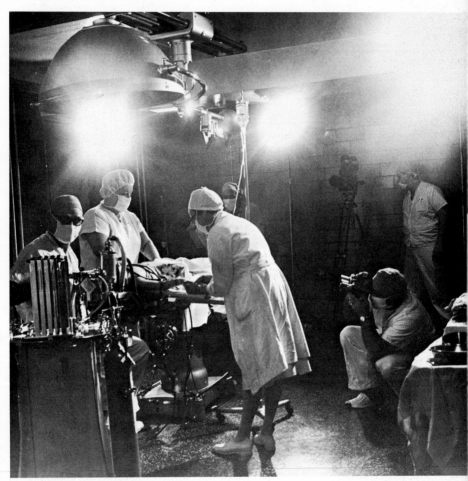
A cameraman covers surgical procedure for an *NBC* news feature

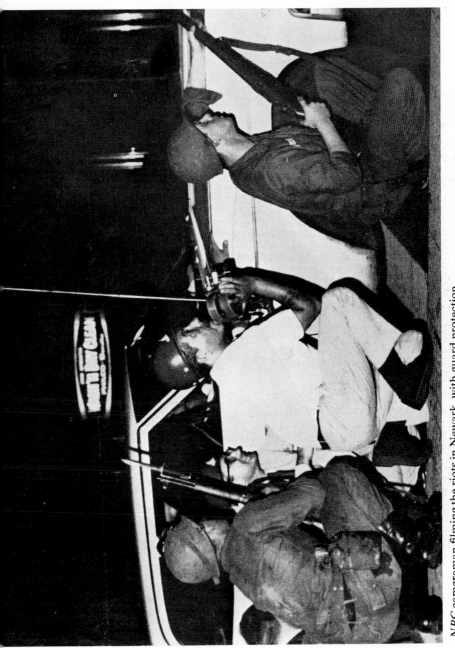

NBC cameraman filming the riots in Newark, with guard protection

Courtesy Michael Fales

Pictures of the Tacoma Park railway station depot after the big fire

Index	
Business	22
Classified	...63-77
Comics	80-84
EDITORIAL	...34
Night Clubs	...62
Obituaries	20
TV-Radio	..78, 79
Sports	36-43
Theaters	...46-48
Women's	...51-61

The Washington Daily News

CITY EDITION   **THURSDAY, AUGUST 17, 1967**

1013 13th St. N.W. (20005) DI. 7-7777   *Second Class Postage at Washington, D. C.*
46th Year—No. 242   *Published Daily Except Sunday*

Weather

Partly cloudy and
warm thru Friday.
High in upper 80's.
Low in upper 60's.

5 a. m. 70
9 a. m. 72

5¢

Fire Wrecks Historic Takoma Park Depot

Page 3

Station Burns

The Takoma Park railroad station in Northeast Washington, built just before the turn of the century, was gutted early yesterday by a fire that may have been set by vandals. The photo above shows how the building looked from the inside afterward and at right is an exterior view. The Baltimore & Ohio Railroad discontinued using the station ten years ago, but trains have been stopping to pickup Washington commuters from its platform.

By Harry Naltchayan—
The Washington Post

Joe Vadala, *NBC News* Cameraman, shooting at the Aswan Dam

Cy Avnet, *NBC News* Cameraman, on location

Author George Gordon with Don Hackel, *ABC* White House Reporter in the Rose Garden

Bruce Cohen (right), *ABC*, Washing with his news director

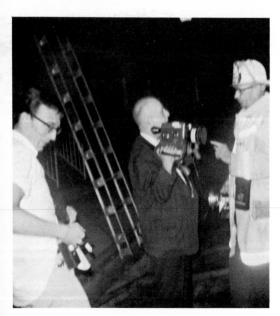

Larry Krebs, *WMAL-TV* Washington Correspondent, covering Tacoma fire

Author Irving Falk (left) with Ted McDowell, Director of News, *WMAL-TV*

Saigon, Moscow, Bonn, Rome, Paris and London. We also have an African bureau that operates out of London. This means that in each one of these places CBS maintains an office, a staff of some kind and at least one — sometimes many more — correspondent stationed there permanently. We also employ 'stringers,' who are on permanent call to us, more or less, in places where we can't afford a full bureau. Don't quote me exactly because the number changes, but I guess we have between seventy-five and eighty 'stringers' stationed around the world, all on call for CBS-TV if we need them. Each one is competent to get us news stories — and usually news film — and transmit it back here to home base if we need it.

"An assignment editor needs a firm grip on every aspect of the international situation, and I'm not exaggerating when I say that I spend twenty-four hours a day on this job. So does Marshall. Maybe we're at our desk for eight hours, but our responsibility for activating all of CBS news sources goes on around the clock. Remember the time differentials between New York and the other major cities of the world! Those differences don't reflect our work day. At this level of network operations, both Marshall and I have to think in global terms — and Saigon at 3:00 A.M. may seem as near as Montreal does right now if our major news story of the day is coming from Vietnam."

Marshall explained further. "Only recently we've broken down our TV assignments to 'domestic' and 'foreign' coverage, and Bob and I are the foreign chiefs. We've both also had experiences with each other's jobs. Bob worries about news, and I worry about film — or getting pictures, somehow, to the United States for network transmission. But that doesn't stop us from worrying about each other, and each other's jobs either! The two are integrated, but they take two men to direct them. We don't travel much ourselves. Last year I traveled some eighty thousand miles checking out our operations. For a foreign newsman, that's nothing! It's good for us to get out of this cow barn now and then to spin around the world—once a year, at least.

"How are TV crews assigned to keep their eyes on the ever-changing international situation?"

"My job is mostly covering *hard* news: stories as they break, not features or documentary stuff," Bob Little explains. "But I have to bear in mind what camera crews are assigned where to do *all* our coverage, because if a hard news story breaks near where we have a crew doing, let's say, a feature on African lions, I can rush them up to the newsfront. Suppose a cameraman is working with a correspondent in Rome, and a revolution breaks on the island of Cyprus. I don't know exactly what the Rome shooting schedule is, but I try to free a cameraman there to go with, say, Winston Burdett to Cyprus. If he's too busy, maybe I pick up another cameraman in Stuttgart, Germany—that is, if he gets along with Burdett. Off they go to Cyprus, and the Rome man can keep working on his documentary.

"But," Marshall Davidson interrupted, "if the President of Italy dies, our Rome cameraman immediately quits his documentary and covers the local story with a Rome correspondent. Of course, we usually have a number of cameramen on call in Rome, but, understand, our people don't ask for assignments. We try to give them the kind of jobs they like—and do—best, but TV news coverage is directed from this desk here in New York.

"Assignments are only one problem. Getting the news or the story on the air is one thing. Getting film onto TV is another. Example: Remember when those Egyptian oil tanks blew up about a year ago? Well, we got some of the first films of the explosions. The film was put on a rinky-dink European airline that would get to London too late to make transmission by the Early Bird Satellite. It stopped in Frankfurt, Germany, but no laboratory in Frankfurt was able to process color film. So what we did was send the film to Cologne, where there is a color lab, by charter plane, then send a girl from Bonn to wake up the film technician in Cologne to develop the thing, because it was 3:00 A.M. by then in Europe. Then we had to arrange to have the film run through Cologne's TV facilities and onto a transatlantic satellite feed to the U.S.A.! And we had about four minutes to decide all this!"

We asked Bob and Marshall what kind of people made the best overseas TV correspondents and cameramen. They both started answering at once. Marshall's bass voice faded as Bob Little's thoughtful answer emerged from the confusion.

"The most effective man overseas," he said with the assurance of an old-time college professor, "is a mature, intelligent person, totally capable of going out, working and solving problems on his own. He has got to be able to stand on his own feet—alone, and frequently without direction from his superiors. Sometimes a cameraman has to be his own correspondent, director, producer, reporter, con-man and travel agent. As the ground rules change—as news breaks—he has to shift with the rules without instructions."

Marshall broke in. "That's the secret! It's true of everyone—correspondents, cameramen, everybody! Overseas, a man like Joe Masraff in Paris, for instance, has a command of what I'd call 'international well-being.' I can tell Joe he's going to Tokyo tomorrow, for instance, and he knows the hotels, he knows the people, how you tip, local customs, which guy to see to get the 'inside dope' and which palms to grease, and which to stay away from. And he knows the same things about most places in Africa or Sweden, or any place. Like most of our people, he can roll with the punches and roll with the story. Juergen Neumann is another man of this stripe who works for us in Europe and Africa. He's a German who started at CBS ten years ago, worked in Vietnam for a year and was Tokyo staff cameraman, then to Bangkok, to Europe, to Mexico, and back to Europe again. He's lived this stuff for a decade, and there's darn little he doesn't know about covering foreign news.

"A correspondent and a cameraman. This is a team! They have to be adaptable people, people who can get along with each other in the middle of Europe or in Rio de Janeiro. Take Joe Masraff and our African correspondent, Frank Kearns. They spent six to eight months at a time in the past few years in darkest Africa. Boy, they never ran into anything like modern plumbing or a bed for long periods of time, and they just had to learn to live with each other and like it under these conditions. They had to be compatible. And, in addition to these unbelievable living conditions, they had to turn out stories, get the darn things photographed and written and in a can and on airplanes where they can do CBS some good."

Bob nodded. "This is why an overseas TV news story is so much more than just compatible words and pictures. We've had good cameramen and good correspondents who just couldn't get along in cities like Vienna—now there's a place you'd think it's easy to live in—so we had to change the teams around. Not only cameramen and correspondents, but also sound men, where and when we could use them."

"All three must know how they are going to cover the action, must take into consideration the correspondent's own basic approach to the story and know what each one can contribute. Then they must decide jointly how they are going to get it, and what they want the end product to be.

The correspondent is the head of the team; his word is final, and his judgment is critical. He has the ultimate responsibility for the quality of the work done. The approach, how he writes it, the angle, the treatment — these are all matters that we leave to the correspondent's judgment. What can I tell a working newsman from my assignment desk in New York? He's the man on the scene, not me, and the point of view has to come from the location of the news source — not from 57th Street."

What's a typical day like at the CBS news desk?

Bob Little raised his hand like a policeman stopping a fire truck. "Can't do that!" he replied. "No day is typical."

Marshall agreed. "A high-pressure day for me is when you worry about getting the footage you have — or the story — on the air. And I worry about that *every* day. Worry is typical — some days more than others. There are other kinds of high-pressure days, but getting reporters to stories and stories to the TV screen sums up the entire hassle. Our big problem is how you best create, and then maintain, an organization which gives you the capability of being able to make a strategic decision in those four minutes I mentioned and not be sorry you did later. And we have competition, because men just as capable as we, are sitting at the assignment desks at the other networks; solving the same problems their own ways, which we just hope isn't better than ours."

A frown came over Bob Little's face. "There are certain things you almost continually do to change the organization, but you always wonder if you are changing it correctly, or how a decision *today* will effect your news covering potential in the long run. Are you making a decision today which is going to kill you a year from now? Short-term problems either work out or they don't. Long-term mistakes at which you fail send you over to NBC to ask if they have a job for an experienced assignment editor!" Bob raised his crossed fingers. "Good luck so far!"

What percentage of actual film shot gets onto network TV at CBS? Neither Bob nor Marshall wanted to answer the question.

"It varies," Marshall said, and Bob nodded. "The amount of film shot on any foreign story really doesn't count. You can go out and, let's say, they've just put the Prime Minister of an Arab nation in jail, and the only film we have of him is walking from the palace to a paddywagon. We'll use all of it, no matter what it looks like. But if we get the complete coverage of a Senator's trip to Vietnam, or a speech that the President of the United States makes overseas, we'll have it *all* on film, but obviously we can't use the whole thing or more than a fraction of it. We may, under those circumstances, use three and one-half minutes out of twelve thousand feet of film! It's the nature of the beast. You cover everything you can get, and you use whatever you've got that fits into a news broadcast!"

At this point, Bob Little got angry at a slight criticism we made that TV covered the news only superficially.

"If you're implying that the average citizen has to depend upon any one medium — say television — for all his foreign news, you're wrong. Dead wrong. TV doesn't work that way, and people don't work that way. How much foreign news the average citizen gets from TV or the newspapers or newsmagazines is your job, professor. You go out and tell us! That's the kind of research a university should be doing, not a TV network.

"I don't think that any intelligent person in our day and age can get all his foreign news — or any news — from any one medium and get a proper picture, and that includes the best newspaper printed in the country. We don't claim that TV covers the whole story. It can't. It does what it does best! Other media do other things."

Suitably pinned down now, Bob Little was asked exactly *what* kind of foreign news TV does cover best! He said nothing for thirty seconds. Then Marshall exploded. "It covers ceremonies—funerals and coronations best! Any pompous ceremony: a state funeral, a wedding, a—"

Bob interrupted. He had been thinking. "No. Don't say that. Any medium covers a staged event well, where everybody knows what's going to happen. But take the war in Vietnam. Here is a situation where TV film cameramen have as much access to actual events as any place else in the world. There are problems involved, but we have top personnel over there with our fighting men. We have a functioning news bureau which is efficient and well operated. Here we do best what we can do—what we can do better than any of the written media. We can show, we can give the sounds, the sights and the words of a terrible war, not as separate elements but put all together as they *are*. That's the point. We don't edit our coverage from headquarters or match silent film with stock sounds and narration. We shoot everything, sound *and* picture, in color, on the spot. And the correspondent who brings the story in has seen it with his own eyes. And because of this we —that is, TV news—can tell the story of what is happening at the Vietnam front better than any other medium."

"For the big picture," continued Bob, "of course, you don't get the entire perspective of the war and what it means to the people of the U.S.A. But do you get that from a single newspaper column or editorial or a single story in a picture magazine? Of course not! To get the complete story, you have to view the entire CBS output over a period of months, maybe even years.

"Then you have to consider our 'special' broadcasts on different aspects of the war. We intend them to fill in the partial pictures that our daily news reports paint. I think, often, people are too critical of isolated efforts of TV news coverage that admittedly—especially, maybe, in foreign news—is incomplete or even distorted. But why can't TV be judged the way the other news media are? Not by isolated instances, but by the *total* job they do."

Marshall picked up the point. "When we think we need a special program, we will then advise Dan Bloom, our bureau chief now in Vietnam, by cable to notify all personnel going to such-and-such a place that we're thinking of doing a special show of some kind on a certain aspect of the situation and to shoot with the 'special' in mind. We also ask him to keep us posted as to what he thinks of the 'special' possibilities. Then our full-hour documentary will be made up not only of daily film clips we've already used in daily newscasts, but new material ordered specifically for the purpose of clarifying for the viewer a complicated news picture."

We asked both Bob and Marshall if they felt that, in any way, they were not covering foreign stories that are important, that the viewers of CBS-TV deserved to see but do not. Both were candid, more so than we had expected.

"Yes," said Bob. "There is a world of stories that we *cannot* cover as we feel we should. Our major obstacle is that we're not given access; we're simply not let in! The freedom of the press is a concept that exists pretty much in the United States alone. Take Red China! We get a story from there once in a blue moon."

"Logistics!" Marshall added. "Lugging equipment around. We're on the threshold of solving that problem, however. The miniaturization of equipment and the development of more satellite systems will open up new dimensions for overseas TV news. In a few years we'll be able to put a story from Cape Town, South Africa (where we're not even allowed to have a bureau at present), on the air, in color and live. I say three years from now!"

Bob nodded. "But plain logistic limitations on TV news are nothing compared to political problems, bureaucracy and red tape overseas, even in countries that are supposed to be democracies. Don't forget that many people and many governments are afraid of the truth — are afraid of giving the press free access to news sources. Logistic problems can be solved — or will be. But these other draw-backs just can't be eliminated as long as people are afraid of the press or afraid of truth. Here at CBS we try to get around these problems whenever we can by assigning men to overseas jobs who are able to use their ingenuity and brains and nerve and experience to get their stories back home accurately — and fast!"

Marshall nodded. "We're doing pretty well. But the world today is the size of a golf ball, and some days some parts of it seem to be millions of light years away! Until the press is free and reporters have reasonable access to important information everywhere, I'm afraid CBS-TV's overseas operation will leave something to be desired. But we are not alone, my friend; we are definitely not alone!"

11

Meet the Chief Foreign Correspondent

Charles Collingwood's name takes you straight back to on-the-spot radio's greatest hour: World War II, and the period immediately before and after it. At the age of fifty, he's a living legend around CBS, one of the last of the correspondents in the newscasting team the late Paul White put together under the war clouds over Europe.

Collingwood recalls the time, more than a quarter of a century ago, when he joined CBS. The place was London, the same city in which he lives, and that he still loves. He remembers those exciting days, his own early twenties and the century's thirties, briefly and without sentimentality. "I went to the university there just before the war," he recalls. "I was at Oxford. And I came down to London to work for five pounds a week — about twenty-five dollars in those days — for the United Press. Then Ed Murrow hired me, right there in London, for CBS."

If Charles Collingwood wears lemon-yellow shirts, blue suspenders and red-and-blue-striped ties to look youthful, he doesn't need to. There is no gray in his sandy hair, and he has gone to neither paunch nor jowl. One could easily misjudge his age by fifteen years, and, like many small, lithe men, he gives you the impression of boundless energy, a tightly coiled spring, a well-honed and sharpened nervous system, and a keen intellect. To think of Collingwood as an "old-timer" is difficult when you talk to him. But he is well aware of the years he has spent in harness. "In the twenty-seven years I've spent with CBS, I never had more than three weeks away from broadcasting's pressure tank," he explains as if apologizing. But it's obvious that Charles Collingwood has worn well on the job.

This is Collingwood's story, however, and not a biography. That will come later, if and when Collingwood himself chooses. It is his story about what it's like to be the CBS-TV (and radio too) Chief Foreign Correspondent — or Chief European Correspondent. Collingwood does not seem to know which title fits best. So let's have him tell it to us in his own words, the way it looked to him back in the first few days of 1968, when a lot of fresh, new calendars hung on the walls of all the TV news bureaus around the world.

"I originally was stationed in Paris for this job, but headquarters were moved to London for technical reasons that should interest anybody concerned with foreign TV coverage these days. The change had to do with the nature of modern communications and the operation of national TV — in Europe, at least.

"You see, when you're a foreign correspondent for an American network, you have to rely largely on local broadcasting facilities, in many cases. In France, that is ORTF, the *Organisation de Radiodiffusion-Television Française.* In England, it's the British Broadcasting Corporation, and so on. Remember now, that French and

British correspondents in this country use the studio facilities of CBS, NBC and ABC. So it works both ways. In Europe, CBS *has* to use theirs.

"Well, when satellite communications began, this dependence upon national TV networks increased. Then we had to use their control rooms, technicians and a tremendous amount of equipment. Now, French TV is nationally owned and controlled and is not competitive with any other TV service. That means that it suffers from bigness, bureaucracy and self-satisfaction, and it is not as reliable as a competitive TV organization like the English BBC, which is given a run for its money (or the taxpayer's money) by British commercial TV. The standards of British TV are comparable to ours, also — standards of excellence, of flexibility, of being able to improvise to meet difficult situations.

"We found that we were having too many troubles with our satellite transmission from our Paris bureau. So I moved my office over to London — without regrets, because I've told you how much I enjoy living in London — where we could rely, mainly, on the BBC, although also, in some ways, on the commercial TV.

"So anyway, my office is now established there, right in BBC headquarters. Because I'm based in London, that doesn't mean that I don't get the chance to cover stories all over Europe — or anywhere in the world when I'm needed. I've been to Vietnam sixteen times since 1960, and I think CBS got a little bit embarrassed introducing me from Saigon, for instance, as our Chief European Correspondent. So that's the reason I'm a Foreign Correspondent now, although Europe is my main beat.

"Professionally, the job of a foreign correspondent is pretty complicated these days. It started with the advent of television and continues apace with the more intensive coverage we have tended—over the past decade, particularly—to give foreign news. The American viewers have been responsible for this, I think. They want more information about other nations and our international problems, and the TV networks have had to provide it. Also, in the old, pre-TV days, correspondents used to cover their own areas almost exclusively. The Paris man would just cover France, and so on. That's changed now, mostly because of jet air travel; and it's changed for the better, I think. We're not entirely interchangeable parts, but we're called upon to go to all sorts of places, particularly those of us who are senior correspondents.

"I was in Israel for the war there. I went to Turkey to cover the Pope's visit. Coincidentally, I ran into an earthquake! I run off to Germany or Paris or anywhere as if they were spots down the street—which they are when you travel by jet these days. I may be covering a story in Paris while our Paris man, Peter Kalisher, may be off in Spain. He came to Israel, for instance, while Winston Burdett, our Rome man, went to Egypt during the Arab-Israeli war. So we all move around quite a lot now.

"Why does Charles Collingwood have to go to these places when CBS has plenty of younger—and maybe smarter—men to cover the action? Well, that's a complicated question to answer and still sound modest. But facts are facts. I've spent a considerable part of my tenure at CBS abroad. I do know people: foreign leaders, key people in ministries, people in business, education, the arts. I know our own embassy people; many of them are now of my generation—that is, the senior people.

"You know—in some ways, I'd like to pursue the more analytic, contemplative approach to world problems, like my colleague, Eric Sevareid, in Washington. But we're very short-handed. We're thin on the ground—every network is — when it comes to finding skilled, experienced foreign correspondents who know their way around — both around the territory, wherever it is, and the ropes of electronic journalism, particularly TV. How many of us are really competent, these days, to cover breaking news stories and, *at the same time*, bring something of a broader, analytic, historical dimension to TV news coverage? Not too many.

"Some assignments, I suggest myself. Some I do on my own initiative. On the other hand, the assignment people in New York or the producers of a particular news program will suggest a story that they want covered. It is, of course, within my option to refuse any assignment, but I seldom do. At heart, I'm a reporter, and a reporter does what his superiors tell him, even if he doesn't need to.

"Not that I'm indispensible, nor do I imagine that some of our younger people can't do as well or better on a story than us old-timers. But I think I can be objective about this: an experienced man brings two things to his work, and they aren't qualities you get from books or learn in a year — or maybe *ten* years. One, I can bring my own education in the crucible of experience; I've already been to most of the places I cover. If I haven't been somewhere, it's pretty certain that I've covered similar stories, allowing me to relate what's going on now to the flow of contemporary history and predict, fairly reliably, possible consequences. Second, after twenty-seven years in radio and TV, I've become better known than newer men. People are familiar with me, and that means, to a certain degree, viewers at home have, hopefully, come to trust what I say, simply because they've seen and heard me before. You can get a bad reputation fast; a good one takes time to develop.

"One thing is certain. TV is the most difficult news medium to work in that has yet been invented. It's mechanically more difficult, more cumbersome; it involves more people and uses more skills and puts more burdens on correspondents than either radio or the press. A TV correspondent is an executive and a squad leader and a strategist as well as a reporter. The logistics of getting your film where it's going, processing and all of these things put unbelievable demands on you. A radio correspondent just has to write his piece, get to a station and broadcast it—period. Someone writing for a newspaper has got only one piece to do which he can file at *his* convenience, although often he's up against a deadline.

"But in TV, we must work according to the New York clock, which is further distorted by the requirements of airlines which operate on local times. Moreover, on most stories, you are doing *both* TV and radio. This means that you are working by New York time, as distorted by problems of shipping in the transmission of TV coverage, while your radio report gets to New York *immediately.* So you find yourself covering the same story several times a day and at all hours of the day or night. The only other news operation comparable to overseas broadcasting is a press wire service for some reason, but they don't have to lug around all the junk we do or worry about shipping schedules.

"Also, on TV coverage you run into problems because of a central fact of news coverage: some important parts of a breaking story simply cannot be shown. Take a cabinet meeting. What are you going to do about a cabinet meeting? Well, one thing is that you can stand outside the door and talk; that's what a lot of us have to fall back on. You can take pictures of the cabinet members going in and coming out. Great! They are invariably dull pictures. But you can't get your lens into the meeting. Now, a newspaper man who has been briefed by a government officer as to what went on during the session—he can write quite a lively story about it. But let me tell you that it's bloody hard to make it a lively story for TV!

"Another thing you can do is interview somebody. But, because there is a time lag of anywhere from twelve to thirty-six hours between the time you do the interview and the time it's shown on American TV, you have to be absolutely certain that it will still be relevant to other news breaking around it. For instance, when I covered the Khartoum-Arab Summit meeting, where Nasser and King Hussein of Jordan were trying to pick up the pieces after the Israeli victory, I was at a loss. There I was, continually tempted to shoot interviews with these leaders, but inevitably they were concerned with what went on that day. But they wouldn't get back to the network in America until that day's story was already dead, having been reported by radio, the newspapers and verbally with still photographs, probably, on TV—in my case, by Walter Cronkite. So an interview from overseas usually can't be too closely identified with major breaking news stories, unless it happens to be from a Western capital city, where you can feed it to the U.S.A. by satellite transmission for that same day's showing. In that case, it has to be important and substantial enough to justify the high costs of satellite transmission.

"There are things that TV can show magnificently, however. Obviously, a major event of almost any kind —the outbreak of a war, tensions, riots, demonstrations and all sorts of events—presents pictorial aspects which are natural for the TV camera. An important story imposes itself on you. You don't create it! Let me tell you exactly what I do—how it works.

"First, I try to familiarize myself as much as I can with the story *before* I get to my destination. Second, unless it's something that happens before I get out of the airport, in which case you shoot what you see, you go to official sources of information. Take the recent crisis in Cyprus, for instance. You go to see President Makarios' spokesman, whoever he is. You go to see Mr. Belcher, the American ambassador. You go to see a representative of the Turkish Government, if you can find him. You go to see the United Nations man. You cover *those* people — officials.

"Third, if you've been there before, perhaps you have other sources. You try to dig beneath these offical statements. What's the real meaning of what you've been told, of what conflicts — or doesn't conflict? When you've begun to get all this into your head, you may be able to pick out the *meaningful visible* things that you can photograph. This might be a UN patrol. You learn that Greek Cypriot lines have formed outside a village occupied by Turks. Here is a point of tension which you can actually show, which *dramatizes* and *symbolizes* all the tension on the island!

"Almost always you'll find significant symbols of the story you are covering. You don't create them, you locate them. Another instance, now: in the Mid-East war last June, between the Arabs and Israel, as the tension began to mount, I arrived in Israel about two weeks before the actual onset of hostilities. Things were getting hot. The UN had been ordered out and had agreed to leave. There was a feeling everywhere of growing anticipation! How do you illustrate a feeling?

"Here's what we did. I went to an Israeli-held border post on the Gaza strip, the closest one to the Arab lines. It happened that here you could actually see former UN barracks with Israeli and Arab troops who had occupied them moving around inside them! So there I stood on this border — with signs posted saying, 'Beware: Border,' and barbed wire barracades — and right behind me were clearly marked UN headquarters now occupied by the Palestine Liberation forces and the Egyptian Army. *That* really described the anatomy of the crisis at the moment! All our moving pictures of the scene needed were brief description from me, and a little background on what this implied for the days ahead! It was perfect on-the-spot coverage for TV.

"Of course there's competition, and often it's very good. I'm rarely the only twenty-seven-year man on the scene. The others are trying to beat me. I'm trying to beat them. Given an even start, you do the best you can, but you don't always win. Competition keeps you awake, though. Sometimes we all turn up at the same place; that often happens. You just try to be more imaginative in what you shoot, more telling in what you say, and more compelling, perhaps, in the way you say it, if you can be. And the competition, naturally, tries to do the same thing.

"Let's get back to London for a minute, shall we? Remember, being a foreign correspondent isn't all dashing around the globe covering conflicts. Mostly, it's routine — never dull, but routine. So suppose I sketch for you what an average day at the London CBS is like for one Charles Collingwood. How's that?

"Because there is five hours' time difference between London and New York, my day tends to start a little later and go on a little longer — sometimes much longer — than at home. Let's say, all unsuspecting, I arrive at my office at about 10:30 A.M. , looking forward to being home at, say, 7:30 P.M. or so.

"The first thing that happens when I get in is that there's a cable from CBS radio telling me they would like me to do a broadcast at noon, our time, on the British problem with their pound sterling currency. They would also like any short subjects that I can give them for other news broadcasts. So I start thinking about this; having already read the newspapers at home, I browse the wire service ticker-tapes and catch up with things. Then, I suppose, I telephone the spokesman for the British Treasury, a man named Chaim Raphael, but everybody calls him 'Rab.' So I ask him, 'Rab, what's the Chancellor of the Exchequer going to do about the pound? What are the pressures? What's the meaning of this or that? What do you think of so-and-so's article in the *Financial Times*? What are the implications of this for the dollar?'—because you have to think in terms of American problems to make the story meaningful for our listeners in the United States.

"I get the story pretty well blocked out in my head, and, just as I start to write it, the Telex—instant communication—begins to chatter from New York! I am informed that there has been a story out of Finland, and color film of it is being shipped to London. They want a satellite feed on it, and they want me to arrange that! And, since they are unfamiliar with the story, will I call the cameraman in Finland who shot it and find out about it and write and voice a narration for it. So then we have to get down to the BBC to arrange details. I put our office manager and a secretary on that. Then I find someone to set up a cutting room, figure out a way to get the film snatched from the plane, processed, edited, a spot-sheet drawn up, and arrange to screen it so that I can write the narration and know, at least vaguely, what I'm talking about.

"By this time, it's, say, 11:30 A.M., and I have a radio show to do in half-an-hour. So I write the thing about the British pound, and I remember that there's been an outbreak of foot-and-mouth disease among the cattle in Devonshire. This I recall, perhaps, from reading the morning papers. So I think: well, that will be an interesting short spot. So I give them a thirty-second piece on foot-and-

mouth disease. And maybe there's been another bank rob-
bery; the English are always robbing banks, and colorfully,
too! So I give them a quick half-minute on that also — all
radio, mind you.

"Then I race downstairs. We broadcast on the floor
below. We've managed to set up our own little overseas
radio control panel and microphone, which is so foolproof
that even *I* can operate it without danger. I get through to
New York and give them these pieces. Then back upstairs.

"It's 12:30 P.M., and now I first begin to look at my
mail. I'm likely to find anything. For instance, the New
York office wants to know whether I've ever worked with a
particular cameraman whom they're thinking of hiring. Or
there's a problem about the office accounts. Or — I don't
know what. Anyway, I'm an administrator, until I manage
to sneak out for lunch between 1:30 and 2:00 P.M.

"After lunch — a short one, usually — I turn to another
kind of project, probably, that I've been working on for
several days. That is, a feature TV story for a news special
or a documentary show. Let's say it has to do with a London dock strike. We've maybe got some of the pieces of it
put together, and now I have to run out with a camera crew
to the docks on the river to film something. We do that,
and I get back to my office late in the afternoon. At this
point, I usually get around to telephoning my wife and
telling her I won't be home for dinner because we have a
10:30 satellite feed. She accepts the fact that it's more
important to feed satellites than to feed me. So someone
gets me a sandwich.

"Now the film from Finland, processed and cut, suddenly emerges. I view it, knock something out, revise the
order of a few shots, and then off we go to the BBC studios. I write a narration for the Finland film and tape a

'voice over' piece for it—all in a race against time, because we want to get it to New York on that 10:30 P.M. satellite feed in time for the CBS evening news program. Since I'm responsible for the operation, I hang around until the feed is completed and New York sends word that both the audio and video have come through in good shape. If something has to be redone, you see, I'd better be there to do it myself. And you don't take anything for granted with transmissions like these.

"If I'm lucky, I get home by 11:30, which isn't a bad working day for an overseas TV correspondent—twelve or thirteen hours. But I hope you noticed that I picked a day when everything went *right*. On the days things go wrong, the picture is different, but never twice in quite the same way. What I've described is a normal day in *London*. It started there and ended there.

"One of the problems, you've got to realize, is that there's an unbelievable amount of uncertainty in the life of a foreign correspondent these days. Something may happen at any time, anywhere in Europe, and, in my position, for reasons I've explained, I am not in a position to pick up telephones and tell other people to cover it for CBS. I am often asked to cover it myself. And there's an old saying that if you want something done right, you do it yourself. So I go. Dinner parties, engagements, theater tickets and other obligations are forgotten. My luggage, incidentally, is always packed. It's packed this minute—"

For the first time, Collingwood's voice broke. His eyes covered with a mist, and he looked at us with a smile that somehow wrinkled his forehead. He seemed unsure of himself now, as if he wanted us to say something. He continued uncertainly.

"I don't know whether they told you or not, but I'm

about to take a sabbatical leave—a *one-year* holiday, a year off. I start this coming Sunday; that's just four days from now, on January 12, 1968.

"I intend to do nothing; no plans—mostly, I suppose, because I'm tired. I don't know what it's going to be like after even a month, and in all honesty, I'm a little frightened. I've made no commitments whatsoever, including none to myself, because I'm not about to unload one set of obligations and deadlines to assume voluntarily another set. First, I'm going to Mexico for the winter, primarily because the sun shines there. And after that, I don't know. Believe me, I *really*, simply don't know.

"Maybe this is wrong. Probably this is the wrong approach! I might have been better off—" Collingwood stopped.

"My life has been planned or subject to the whims of news and fate for so long that I just don't want to have any deadlines! I don't want to have to be anywhere at any particular time. We'll see how it works. And, right now, I'm certainly not thinking of anything past the year and the vacation ahead.

"But I want to try to pull these twenty-seven years together and take a clear fix, if I can, on the future. Although I've been around here for all those years, I'm not all that old, and I'm certain there are plenty of good years ahead. I want to think about how to spend them. Anyway, it's about time I had a vacation, just lie in the sun and let someone else cover the action for a while. Don't you think so?"

We do! Have a great year, Charles Collingwood, and be good to yourself! We'll be seeing you again—soon.

12

Faces on the TV Tube

One thing that the well-known newscasters at CBS agree on concerning overseas news coverage is that it's no bed of roses.

Nor is it entirely a bed of thorns. Every correspondent to whom we spoke seemed ready to leave at a moment's notice for an overseas assignment. Mike Wallace, for instance, whose beat is usually New York but who has done his tour of duty on foreign soil, described to us enviously the jobs of Bernard Kalb and Marty Fromson. Kalb and Fromson have prime assignments, according to Wallace. The former is stationed in Hong Kong and the latter in Bangkok, but each alternates with the other on a monthly basis, covering the Vietnam war from Saigon — and other, less secure places.

Relative old-timers like Dick Hottelet sometimes find themselves covering "overseas" beats like the United Nations, a taxicab ride away from the CBS-TV studios in New York. Hottelet is the kind of man who can look you straight in the eye and claim that the worst risks he ran covering World War II in Europe for CBS Radio were the potential traffic accidents he was exposed to following the front lines of battle across Europe with the allied armies! His "foreign" assignment at the UN seems interesting enough, but you sense a restless yen for adventure when he talks about his work.

"The action at the United Nations," says Hottelet, "is a rather formal, repetitive one—a minuet whose visible motions are always the same. The Security Council meeting is always in the same chamber, and so forth. So, pictorially, we are at a great disadvantage on TV. Accordingly, the task of covering the UN is certainly a challenging—and sometimes impossible—job, because it's always the same picture.

"But," he continues, "to the extent that TV is interested in *ideas* and in *content*, of course, the UN is a cross-section of international life today, endlessly varied, even though the same sort of problems repeat themselves year after year. Covering the UN is like covering a microcosm of the world, with all the problems that that entails." He added wistfully, "Except the problems of travel, distance and time for the reporter, which, I guess, is a blessing."

Hottelet takes a long-range view of the role of foreign correspondents, the kind of view which, he claims, is helpful in covering tough assignments like the UN in New York. "When I became a reporter nearly thirty years ago, I overlapped slightly with what you'd call the 'old school' of foreign correspondents. These were a varied collection of men, some of them the old rough-and-ready types, who are better at a poker game or a night on the town than at an embassy or national capitol. I wouldn't like to name names because it sounds invidious, but for the most part, with exceptions—and some great exceptions—the level of their understanding of international events and their meaning was low, it seems to me. They were adventurers rather than reporters.

"Then, just before and during World War II, I think the intellectual level of these people rose. I think correspondents came into the field — radio and newspapers then — who were better educated, who spoke foreign languages and who were a little more aware of the complexity of foreign news."

Hottelet is a seriously inclined man. He tends always to speak with precision and conviction, qualities that have characterized his work since his first broadcasts, twenty-four years ago. "I'm not entirely certain that all of our, or any other network's, correspondents today are of the caliber I'm talking about. In Vietnam today, for instance, I have *not* been wildly and happily struck by the level of competence of the TV reporters, and my criticism is not only of CBS but is leveled at radio and TV both in the U.S.A. and elsewhere.

"Vietnam started out as a secondary story, and I'm not sure that the younger people who have been sent there to date have kept up the development toward excellence in foreign reporting that was characteristic of the years during and after World War II in Europe. This is an impression I have, but when you think of the hundreds of reporters who have been to Vietnam, I would be hard pressed to name more than five who have distinguished themselves consistently in any manner. I suppose I'm not only thinking here of radio and TV correspondents, but of newspaper and magazine people as well. What we miss is trained, objective reporters in the field."

"Of course, it's a tough assignment out there in the Pacific!" said Hottelet, looking at his watch. "And so is the United Nations. I'm sorry I have to cut the conversation short, but I'm off to my war—on the East River. And don't get the idea that the battle there doesn't sometimes get pretty vicious!" Hottelet was on his way across town.

Mike Wallace does not look at TV overseas newscasting from quite the same scholarly perspective as his colleague. "But, for heaven's sake, don't make me out to be a foreign correspondent," implored the intense, youthful Wallace, puffing on an empty briar pipe. "I'm not. I'm just a reporter who happened to receive a few overseas assignments. And I'm not an authority on the subject. I simply try to give whatever story I'm on the best I have in me, and that's the way it's been since I started in the newspaper game twenty-seven or so years ago!"

Foghorns on the Hudson hooted beyond the windows outside Wallace's office. "Sometimes, though, I get fed up with domestic newsbeats. I spend too much time here in New York City, and, after a while, I feel like a rewrite man rather than a reporter. Then it's about time for me to travel, to see some different faces and different territory. The problem is that when I get overseas, I'm no expert, I'm just a reporter. The only two places where I stayed long enough to feel that I really began to understand the situation were in Vietnam and Israel. And, even so, I'm no expert on either Southeast Asia or the Middle East. That takes years of study and hard work. Other people provide the expertise for CBS, not me. I merely try to provide an exciting story or two—one a day, if possible."

How? Where do the stories come from?

"Well, take Vietnam, for instance. When a correspondent from the home office here is sent out there, most of the time he's pretty much on his own, following his own instincts and doing what he wants in his own way. Certainly he gets cameramen and technicians and all the advice he needs. And our CBS bureau in Saigon is first-rate. John

Flynn, the bureau chief when I was there, was an old Saigon hand and had ideas for stories which were invaluable. So did Seymour Wolen, the assistant bureau chief, who put me on to leads of many kinds that paid off magnificently.

"Then, an attractive girl named Judith Osgood, in her early thirties, was in charge of our research. Now, she knew everybody in Saigon. I think she's just arrived back in the States, but in Vietnam she was invaluable to our correspondents and knew the cast of characters in town, from ambassadors to generals to cab drivers, who might provide the kind of information I needed to set up interesting stories for *both* radio and TV. No reporter lives alone. He always has to depend upon others. But it's his own news sense that guides him in the selection of a story and its treatment."

Wallace's chair squeaked as he leaned forward to fill his pipe. "For a reporter like me, an overseas assignment is a tonic. It helps me to see things in a—well—different perspective or from a different angle than before. Before I went to Vietnam, I suspected that the Saigon Government—and even the Vietnamese Army—was suffering more than its allowable quota of confusion and corruption. Well, at this instant, I still have the conviction that confusion and corruption abound in South Vietnam. But the difference is that I've seen it with my own eyes; I've actually experienced it. It's that seeing and experiencing that the good TV reporter tries to get into his stories. I imagine I succeeded, because CBS used my material on its network telecasts. More important, I'm a better reporter now, because I've been on the scene and looked at, tasted and smelled what that war is all about!"

His pipe still unlit, Wallace was hammering now with his finger on his desk. "But no heroics! I was up front a

number of times, but the front in Vietnam is everywhere — sometimes in the streets of Saigon. Also, I was
'under fire,' but nobody was shooting at *me* in particular.
And the only thing I shot was film! The trick in covering a
foreign story is the same as all news coverage. You want
interesting stories, you want colorful stories and, if possible, you want exclusive stories.

"People usually think of me as an interviewer. Well, I
suppose I made my reputation asking people questions,
and I still do. But there's more to a news story than just
personalities. A great event contains a multitude of elements, the total significance of which a good reporter
knows how to grasp and communicate to others. I've found
that I can't keep on my toes without going out there every
once in a while." Wallace's arm swept in the general direction of the tugboat horns. "Taking your turn as a correspondent in the field clears the cobwebs and brings you to
the heart of the matter, wherever and whatever it is!"

Neither Wallace nor Hottelet looks at the labors of
covering foreign news in quite the way that Walter Cronkite does. They call Cronkite an "anchor man" both on and
off the air, and he looks like an anchor man: impeccably
groomed (except that his famous moustache, which seems
so neatly trimmed on TV, has a shaggy look off camera),
gracious, good-humored and soft-spoken.

"I was a foreign correspondent," recalls Cronkite, "in
the days before I turned into an anchor — in fact, before I
entered broadcasting. It gets in your blood. I nearly
covered the Korean War for CBS when I first joined the
company, but my assignment was changed at the last minute. There's something about foreign correspondents,
though, whether they're broadcasters or print journalists. I
suppose it's a mystique, but once you've worked in an
overseas bureau, you feel somehow close to other foreign

correspondents and can communicate easily with them. At least, you understand their problems in ways that assignment personnel and other stateside newsmen cannot. I flatter myself that some of our overseas people here at CBS think of me in that way and come to me as 'a friend in court,' so to speak. Not every day, of course, but every once in a while."

Cronkite, a surprisingly modest man, added quickly, "Now, don't make too much of that 'friend in court' business! It's just that not too many other domestic newscasters have been as lucky as I have in putting in a good share of overseas service over the years. And also, I guess I've attained," he paused, "a certain amount of maturity which our men overseas appreciate occasionally when they run into problems. That's all."

Now, there was one question we had wanted to ask Cronkite for years, and it took a little nerve to frame it: why had he become CBS anchor man for all of those earth-shattering TV broadcasts over the years and not one of the others in the crop of correspondents employed by the network?

Cronkite smiled and shrugged eloquently. "Dunno!" he replied. "I guess it just happens to be a combination of minor things—no one of them too important, really —coming together in what has been a lucky amalgam. Background is one thing, a pretty extensive one which partly can be translated into 'age'! I've also had an opportunity of working in almost every facet of the news business —newspaper, press service, radio, TV and the whole works—and in a lot of different posts and assignments, from city editor to war correspondent. And, of course, I had the lucky break of getting in on the ground floor of TV news. That was pure luck, naturally."

"I suppose there's another point temperamentally too,"

continued Cronkite reflectively. "I'm not interested in trying to be an authority, a fortune teller, or what they call a 'pundit.' I guess I have pretty much the same feeling working with news that a farmer has working with the soil. I just want to dig around in it and grow what I can, not mine it for oil or gold. Just because I'm in the news business, I try not to kid anybody into thinking that I think I know all the answers. Good grief, I don't even know all the right questions!

"Another thing. I've learned over the years what the limitations of our business are and what problems it presents, and I try to be as honest as I can about these facts of life both with my fellow newsmen and with the TV viewers. Maybe people sense this — anyway, I hope they do." Cronkite stopped and fixed a stern eye on us. "I don't want to overplay this either. You brought up the 'anchor man' question; I didn't.

"Don't forget, there are a number of terrible frustrations in the TV news game, and you have to learn to stand up against them all. *Time* is the major one. First of all, there's a competition with the clock to get on the air at all with a story and to give it the amount of coverage it requires. Second, you've got the problem of telling the news story responsibly in whatever time you've managed to get for it! A minute isn't enough, and sometimes an hour isn't enough. Both of these time problems cause massive frustrations.

"Can you imagine trying to get across in *two minutes* a report on the French position towards the NATO forces, especially when you're an authority to some degree on the subject, like our correspondent in Paris? In a case like this, he's stymied, and I know the problem he's having. He needs at least five minutes to get started and provide background and so forth. But how often do we have five min-

utes on a news show for an explanation of a country's
position on anything? Too many breaking news stories
—many of them much less important than this—force us to
cut our man's 'stand-up piece' down to next to nothing."

Cronkite held up a spiral notebook. "I've just returned
from the Republican governors' conference in Florida.
Well, here are my notes on it. This book is absolutely full
of important material that I gathered over a period of three
days. Fascinating stuff! All of this material is just background for what ends up as a few minutes on the air
—more on radio than TV—but nothing like what I want to
say about that conference and its implication for national
politics. And, frankly, I'll never get to it." He slapped the
pad on his desk. "Background, that's all this is. How do
you like that for frustration?

"Of course, to me, the experience in Florida was invaluable, because now I'm going to be able to discuss all
this background at convention time—you know, during
those long pauses between ballots or during a lull in the
proceedings. But every newsman wants to use the important news he gets now. There's the pressure of time again!
If I had covered that governors' conference simply as a
reporter to broadcast only the tiny bit that I'll be able to
say about it now, why, I'd be chewing my fingernails to the
bone with frustration."

Then Cronkite laughed. "I'm not complaining. Or,
rather, I'm complaining, but certain factors compensate
pretty well for all these shortcomings. TV's great strengths
are twofold. We can introduce the people who are in the
news to the public and make them almost as familiar as
one's next-door neighbor. This is an important and fascinating aspect of TV spot coverage if you think about it. So
many of us, unfortunately, take it for granted that we don't
think. Well, it's a miracle! With TV we can expose the

frauds and 'phonies' and show them to the public for what they are. Senator Joe McCarthy was an example. And we can give some of the fine, worthy and honest men among us (and there are plenty) a chance to be heard and seen. Things don't always work out this neatly, naturally, but that's the direction in which I like to think TV news is heading. When I stop believing that, it will be time for me to quit.

"Then we can take people to places where the news is being made and familiarize them with the whole world. The depth of understanding we gain from a knowledge of how a country, a society, a culture acts on people who make news is an invaluable dimension which TV brings to news coverage that other media do not—or at least do not do as well. For the first time, the audience can see on TV how people in other places are living *today, right now, this minute.* This quality of TV is one I have great faith in, and I think will be extremely significant in the future growth of spot news coverage.

"What I'm saying doesn't only relate to TV, however. All these things are a matter of degree. The *impact* of TV is greater than that of any of the media—print or electronic—and that's why these particular points stand out in importance to me. What we do well, we do much better than the other media. And the problems that force us to operate under handicaps—"

The anchor man shrugged without finishing his sentence.

"Oh, don't misunderstand. I love every part of this business. I love being an 'anchor,' if that's what you want to call me. I'll admit that it's not as exciting today as it was fifteen years ago. Then we were pioneers, and everything was new—and unbelievably exciting! It was a period of 'firsts': the *first* live broadcast from Washington Airport on General MacArthur's return from his Pacific command, for instance. Now that program won't make a page in anybody's history book, but, at the time, we thought it was pretty great stuff!"

The enthusiasm of some well-kept nostalgia lit Cronkite's face. "The *first* transcontinental use of the microwave relay system to cover the San Francisco peace conference! The *first* nationally televised picture," Cronkite hesitated, "of a man going to the washroom! That's a story you don't know, I'll bet."

We said we didn't and we do not bet.

Cronkite explained, "It was back in the late nineteen-forties or early fifties. Andrei Gromyko, the Soviet delegate to the United Nations, was supposed to walk out one night during the American Secretary of State's speech, as a dramatic gesture of defiance against the Western nations. So we were all set to cover him on TV. Sure enough, at one point Gromyko got up, ponderously moved down the long hall and right through it. Doug Edwards was outside reporting: 'A limousine has just driven up, and it's waiting here and there is no doubt that he is walking out.' Then they cut to a shot of Gromyko in the hall, and Doug said, 'Here he comes, the door is just opening, he's in the corridor and — whoops — !' Then the camera followed Gromyko right into the gentlemen's washroom! Gromyko came out later with a sly look on his face, as if to say, 'Who says Russians don't have a sense of humor?'" Cronkite was laughing now.

"It was fun. But I can't complain about TV news today — the excitement of creation, of trying to make this miraculous invention work even better is great. It's a little overwhelming; there are so many angles to it, particularly economic problems within the industry. But none of them keep it from being an interesting line of work, especially for an 'anchor man.'

"And that, gentlemen," concluded Cronkite, "is the way it is!"

13

TV News from Everywhere

On August 10, 1967, the CBS network's evening news program used seven news stories from around the world, as well as more than a dozen other items delivered directly "on camera" by Walter Cronkite. We'll put aside these latter stories, which Cronkite and the CBS news staff in New York select and write from wire services, from files made up by other correspondents and from telephone inquiries.

We'll concentrate on those seven stories, fed by CBS news from Oakland, California; Detroit; Washington; Jacksonville, Florida; Odense, Denmark; Paris; and Saigon, and give you the pertinent details of how and under what circumstances they appeared on CBS news on that average, ordinary Thursday evening.

Jacksonville, Florida: The story from Jacksonville ran for ninety seconds on the air. It began two days before when the CBS Atlanta Bureau Manager learned that Black Power spokesman Rap Brown was to speak to a gathering in Jacksonville the following day.

The bureau manager notified the assistant manager in New York City, and they agreed that they ought to have someone covering this potentially explosive event. As usual, the two correspondents and the two crews operating out of Atlanta were already out on assignment — one in Louisiana, the other in Mississippi. So CBS alerted a camera "stringer" in Miami and hired a reporter from an affiliated station in Jacksonville. But the idea was for the cameraman in Miami to stay where he was, because Brown was scheduled to be tried in a New York court Wednesday morning, and if he were convicted and imprisoned, he would never get to Jacksonville.

That morning, however, the trial was postponed; Brown left for Jacksonville and was due to arrive at 3:30 P.M. Atlanta was notified, and the cameraman and reporter were sent to meet Brown at the airport. On the evening of the ninth, CBS filmed Brown at his scheduled meeting and shipped the film by air to the Atlanta News Bureau.

It got to Atlanta at midnight on Wednesday. The Atlanta bureau manager had made arrangements for its film laboratory to open its facilities in the middle of the night. The film went to the laboratory, where it was processed; from there it was rushed to the studios of the CBS Atlanta affiliate. The bureau manager, along with a local film editor he had hired, were there at the studios.

The editing was finished early Thursday morning. But the story was not ready to go to New York, because two pieces were still missing. During the meeting in Jacksonville, there had been an unexpected confrontation between Rap Brown and Governor Kirk of Florida. The stringer cameraman happened to be changing his film magazine when the meeting occurred! The reporter on the scene thought how lovely it was to be a newspaper reporter — the worst that can happen with your equipment is that your pencil breaks!

The confrontation had, however, been filmed by the CBS Jacksonville affiliate. The network people in New York asked them for it, but they could not (or *would not*) release it until it had been broadcast on their 11:00 P.M. news. That was *one* of the missing pieces!

The Jacksonville affiliate had, in addition, arranged for Governor Kirk, who rarely misses a chance to be on TV, to appear live at its studio for the 11:00 broadcast. CBS news made arrangements to tape-record his remarks for that evening's network broadcast. That was the other missing element!

These two additional pieces were ultimately flown to Atlanta, where the bureau manager and editor got them in hand at 2:10 A.M. The two of them put the story together on film. The bureau manager wrote the script and narrated the story.

At this point, there was no time to transmit the completed story to New York by plane, so it was fed electronically to CBS news headquarters at a quarter past six in the morning—barely in time for the 7:00 A.M. news broadcast. Later that morning, the CBS Atlanta Bureau Manager, who hadn't been to bed in over twenty-four hours, shipped the film itself to New York, where network people edited it and made the ninety-second cut which was used that evening.

Washington, D.C.: The Washington story ran seventy-five seconds on the network news program. It had a deadline problem "due to circumstances beyond the broadcaster's control"—as they always are!

Dan Rather, CBS White House correspondent, was on duty that Thursday morning, when the Executive Director of the President's commission on the current riots called a news briefing to announce a shake-up in the National Guard. Rather was assigned to attend the briefing, discussed it with the CBS news producer in New York and then did a "stand-up piece" in front of the White House.

That was easy enough, and there was plenty of time to make the evening news. But covering TV news just cannot be that simple, and it wasn't! The film was scheduled to be processed by the "jiffy processor" at the CBS Washington Bureau. The processor broke down!

Then began the race against the clock! The film was carried out to the CBS affiliate in Washington for processing and then brought back to the Washington Bureau for editing. It was getting late, and this story was earmarked as the lead story for evening broadcast. At twenty-five minutes past six — the first CBS network news feed begins at 6:30 — the editing process was completed in Washington, and the edited story was fed electronically to New York. It made the lead story on the broadcast — with about four minutes to spare. Incidentally, circumstances like these, which TV journalists learn to expect, illustrate why there must be emergency coverage available in case a story does *not* arrive on time, and why the TV "newspaper" never "goes to bed" until it gets out on the air.

Detroit, Michigan: The Detroit story ran for three-and-a-half minutes on the August 10 evening news. The day before, the newspaper *The Detroit News* ran a story about the alleged murder of a Negro by the Detroit police during the recent riots. The CBS New York assignment manager sent a reporter from the Chicago Bureau and a camera stringer from Montreal to cover the story.

They interviewed a number of people on film, tried unsuccessfully to obtain a police statement, processed the film in a Detroit laboratory and shipped it by air to New

York. So far so good, and time was ample. But Murphy's Law—"if anything can go wrong, it will"—operated inexorably! There was a shipping delay, and the processed film did not get to New York until Thursday morning. It was screened in New York by a producer, who decided that he would not use it unless it was possible to supplement and balance it with a statement from the Detroit police.

The reporter in Detroit was instructed to go after the Detroit police again. Finally he got an interview with the Police Commissioner. Once again, the filmed interview was processed in a Detroit laboratory. But it had to be edited so that it could fit the filmed material already in New York. The CBS news producer in New York, the reporter in Detroit and a film editor from a CBS Detroit affiliate all cooperated in a remote-control editing session. The hour was getting late, and so the edited film had to be fed by telephone company lines to New York, where it was integrated into the film already on hand.

Oakland, California: The story from Oakland ran five minutes and forty-six seconds. It was what TV men call an "enterpriser"—a previously assigned feature on the emotional wounds of Vietnam's soldiers. The story had been suggested by a CBS Los Angeles correspondent. Since it was relatively timeless, it was not subject to normal deadline pressures. But, in TV, when there are no time pressures, there are usually other troubles. And there were.

After the Los Angeles correspondent completed the story and the filmed material reached New York, it was screened by a news producer. He decided that it was not usable because one of the key interviews—and here is a problem that newspapers never have—had been spoiled by a hair which had hung over the camera gate behind the lens when the sequence was photographed.

The Los Angeles correspondent and a crew were naturally instructed to go back and reshoot the interview. This sounds simple enough. But to film the interview again, the camera equipment had to be sent by air from Los Angeles to Oakland. It so happened that an essential piece of the equipment — a battery cable — was somehow mislaid by the airline. A new cable had to be found and flown to Oakland, and the interview was completed and used on the CBS network news program.

Saigon, Vietnam: The Vietnam story was routine. The CBS Bureau in Saigon learned through its Vietnamese reporter that the President of South Vietnam, would hold a news conference on August 9. The Saigon Bureau Manager assigned overseas correspondent Bernie Kalb and a cameraman to cover the conference.

The unprocessed film was shipped by regular jet from Saigon to San Francisco. CBS News always attempts to get at least one important Vietnam story to San Francisco in time to feed it by telephone line to New York for the evening CBS news broadcast. But this particular jet plane did not arrive in San Francisco until 7:00 P.M. New York time on Wednesday, August 9 — too late for the network broadcast that day.

So the film was flown to New York overnight, processed and made available to CBS News early Thursday morning for that evening. If the film had reached San Francisco on an earlier flight on Wednesday, it would have been met by CBS personnel in the Los Angeles Bureau, who would have gone up to San Francisco, processed and edited it there and then fed it by line to New York in time for the CBS News broadcast the same evening — August 9, the day of the conference.

Paris, France: The Paris story involved a satellite feed. It began on July 30 when CBS Foreign Assignment Manager Bob Little, whose hunches are the best in the business (so his colleagues say), suspected that President Charles de Gaulle would soon feel the need to make a TV report to his countrymen about his recent trip to Canada. While there, he had outraged Canadians and Americans alike by practically commanding the French-Canadian population to revolt against their government.

A telephone call by the CBS Paris Bureau to the French press information officials confirmed the hunch. It turned out that de Gaulle was to make a TV report on August 10 at 3:00 P.M. New York time. American broadcasters were not allowed to screen the tape in advance.

If the story was to make the CBS evening news broadcast, therefore, the Paris Bureau had just three and one-half hours to obtain the tape, edit it, translate it, add analysis and reportage and get it to the CBS studio in New York. That meant satellite transmission. It also meant lining up requisite broadcast and production personnel, and arrangements for technical facilities in Paris to edit and translate, to record veteran reporter Charles Collingwood's analysis and to transmit the story to New York.

The main problem CBS faced was that the equipment of the French Government broadcasting organization, ORTF, whose facilities had been used, is insufficient to meet the requirements of *all three* American networks at any one time. Since ORTF operates on a first-come, first-served basis, there was a danger of CBS being excluded entirely. So the Paris Bureau immediately contacted ORTF, got there first and reserved a videotape machine, a live camera and studio facilities. With these in their back pocket, CBS staffers then went to NBC and ABC to arrange for satellite transmission on a pooled basis.

Giving up exclusivity was not an easy decision for the CBS Paris Bureau Manager to make. It turned partially on economics and partially on a desire to remain on a reasonably friendly basis with the competition. CBS decided to pool to save money, yes, but also to pocket a due bill with NBC and ABC if next time *they* got there first. The pool saved CBS two-thirds of the cost of the satellite transmission. Because CBS had managed to tie up the ORTF equipment, NBC and ABC readily accepted the pool.

The networks worked out an agreement that the pool would feed pictures and sound of de Gaulle in French, and, during the period of satellite transmission, which was divided up among the three networks, each would unilaterally feed its *own* supporting material. The CBS material was Collingwood's analysis of the broadcast.

On August 10 at 3:00 P.M. New York time — three and one-half hours before CBS evening network news went on the air — the American network people in Paris had a tape of the entire de Gaulle speech in their hands. They worked on it and agreed in Paris on what portions of the speech were to be included in the pool transmission. It was a case of editing by committee — an unpopular procedure, but one which *works* when the pressure is on.

The edited excerpts were fed by telephone landlines to the satellite ground station at Pleumeur Bodou, then transmitted to the satellite at about 5:00 P.M., received at the ground station in Andover, Maine, transmitted by landline to the telephone company in New York and distributed from there to the three networks. At the same time, a Collingwood "voice over" went by an independent CBS voice circuit directly from Paris to CBS in New York, where it joined up with the pooled tape piece that had arrived by satellite. And so the viewers of CBS News that evening saw and heard the highlights of a de Gaulle speech which had been delivered three and one-half hours earlier in France.

Odense, Denmark: The story from Odense, Denmark,

began at 6:30 A.M. on August 10, when the CBS Foreign Assignments Editor was called at home in New York by the assignment desk. He was informed that one of the wire services had just transmitted a bulletin concerning a train wreck outside Copenhagen.

The assignment editor would normally have thought such a story not worth the effort, but, since he knew that CBS was already using the satellite that day for the pool transmission of de Gaulle, he decided to go after the Odense story. It could easily get a free ride on the satellite transmission of the French President's speech.

So, from his home, he cabled the CBS London Bureau to find out from the European Broadcasting Union what coverage, if any, Danish TV intended to transmit over Eurovision lines—and also to get more details about the accident. At the same time, CBS in New York cabled its Paris Bureau to arrange for appropriate ORTF facilities to record in Paris any story that might be fed over the Eurovision lines.

The London Bureau made various calls, trying to get more details, and finally obtained from the EBU offices in Geneva, Switzerland, a "shot list" of the material that Danish TV planned to feed on the train wreck. The shot list was sent by Telex (teletype) to New York, where a CBS news producer made a tentative decision that it was a newsworthy story. This was later confirmed by the London Bureau when a newsman got to see the coverage.

At this point, at CBS's request, NBC and ABC agreed to include the Odense material in the pool transmission. The story was recorded in Paris from Eurovision lines and was included in the satellite transmission. And that evening, the CBS network evening news audience saw a twenty-three-second film piece of the train wreck—narrated by Walter Cronkite himself in New York.

We have accounted for the *seven* stories used on the broadcast on that *one* Thursday evening in August. Stories that were missed and stories that came in but were not televised were not included so that we could tell about the important events that occurred during those twenty-four hours. This review does not tell of the intense planning in New York for that day: the procedures as film stories arrived and were screened and news judgments made to include or exclude, to edit and to fit each piece into that twenty-three-minute hole, which is all that is available on the CBS evening news program.

14

The Long View from the Top

William R. McAndrew* is President of NBC News and can be found in a comfortable fifth-floor office in Rockefeller Center, whose good taste and decor provide considerable contrast to the functional spareness of the NBC newsroom, located less than one hundred feet away.

Bill's windows look out on Rockefeller Plaza. His green rug has the kind of resilience that you might expect in an executive suite, and set into his bookcase is a panel displaying three TV color monitors, each tuned to a different New York network station. After looking at them for a minute or two, you get the feeling that you want to turn up the volume on all of them at once to discover whether they sound as wild as the three colorful, cavorting picture tubes look.

Some people might be insulted by being called "grandfatherly," but Bill McAndrew is not that sort of man. In the first place, he is a grandfather, and in the second, the

*This interview took place early in January, 1968. Mr. McAndrew died on May 30, 1968.

word would be a just tribute to his lifetime in the news
field, from a job as a ten-dollar-a-week copy boy in the
United Press to the top echelon at NBC and an office with
three color television sets.

What strikes you first about Bill's ideas concerning spot
TV news is his faith in the medium. "Electronic journalism has only just come of age," he comments, "and it has
grown up in a remarkably short time. Take TV's role in
politics. Coverage of the 1952 conventions was the first
really transcontinental TV exposure given these events.
Well, delegates went home and discovered that they were
really *seen* on TV. When they returned to their convention
halls — Republicans and Democrats alike — in 1956, they
paid a good deal of respect to the TV cameras and the
audience back home. In my opinion, the political impact of
TV is growing all the time. Some people look upon this
with fear, afraid that only telegenic candidates will be able
to win elections. Well, I don't agree with them. Electronic
journalism is one of the most penetrating forms of news
coverage we know. It has the potential to tell the *truth*
more accurately than newspapers or magazines or any
other medium. And I'm not afraid of communicating truths
to the public."

Bill leans on his desk and punctuates his words with
taps of his well-manicured fingers on his desk. "Of course,
all broadcasters have obligations of many kinds, and
my job here at NBC is to make sure that we in the news
department meet them. Some of the weeping willies in this
business cry loud and long about the conflict between
commercial interests at the networks and their news departments — that is, entertainment broadcasting, which is
highly profitable, versus news broadcasting, which is not.
Their first assumption is that the two are incompatible, and
this is downright untrue. I think NBC can stand on its

record in this regard. I'm also firmly convinced that administrators who do not understand the realistic conditions of the industry—or college or government agency—for which they work should not be permitted to administrate.

"Many people talk about the impending creation of a Public Broadcasting Service here in the United States. Well, possibly this will come to be, but not by attempting to do the kind of news coverage that the networks do well *right now*. Let the Public Broadcasters try what we *can't do* or are *too timid to do*—only let me tell you that every year, as TV news broadcasting develops, we in the networks are providing mature and controversial kinds of news coverage that we once might have stayed clear of, fearing complaints from sponsors or listeners. That's one thing we have certainly learned: whatever we cover and however we cover it, someone will complain, and you can't please everybody. Again, I ask you merely to look at NBC's record to see the growth and scope of our coverage today, the many and serious problems that we discuss on our news shows and the caliber of the people involved in them."

When asked about TV's future, Bill replies, "It's easier to guess what's not going to happen to TV spot news coverage than what is! I don't think, for instance, that present network news programs will be replaced by this Public Broadcasting System (no matter how good it is) or by a single 'news TV channel' of any kind. I think the networks will continue to develop their individual news operations pretty much as they have in the past, back to the days of radio. Nor do I believe that the networks will work out a continuing pool and slice up the job of news coverage between them. Such a move would be against our monopoly laws, I'm sure, and all of us, including my opposite numbers at CBS and ABC, are too competitive in our approach to this business to cooperate more than occasionally. Also, competition between the networks is good; it keeps us on our toes, and we know it.

"TV will continue to go after the news, wherever it is, and two technical changes will, I think, give us more flexibility. First, I'll guess that we are about due to scrap our present 16-mm film cameras and projectors and substitute super-8-mm for news photography. Second, the advances that are being made in developing easily portable color TV cameras and tape recorders are remarkable. You'll notice these technical changes on your home screens in the near future. Our coverage will be more complete, more accurate and more interesting.

"I also firmly believe that more broadcasting hours in the future will be devoted to TV news. If not more hours, then at least more 'prime time' between 7:00 and 11:00 P.M. on the networks' schedules. I predict this for one reason—and *not* because the present entertainment format between those hours is unprofitable. It is highly profitable. But the people want news—especially, I think, during those peak listening hours. And the people usually get what they want!

"Oh, perhaps we'll start out with a five-minute summary between variety shows. But I won't be surprised if, in the next decade or two, we live to see a full hour of news broadcasting, on one network at least, *every* night during the so-called prime time, both making money and competing profitably with entertainment programs. While most people, it's true, watch TV to relax, our audience is growing up in its tastes, at least at the rate that we in TV are growing more competent to satisfy them! This is a big country, and the potential TV audience for news is enormous—*if* TV can offer it material that competes not only with other news sources, like newspapers and magazines, but with domestic comedies and other entertainment programs as well."

Bill was now standing by his window, looking thoughtfully at the passersby in the street. "Man for man, I'd say that your TV news broadcaster is as dedicated and as talented as any other newsman—and woman—in this country. I'll bet you've come to that conclusion too—on your own, writing this book of yours. Our greatest challenge in the future will be keeping up the caliber of these people—the kind of people you have met in our newsrooms and in other TV newsrooms around the country. Did I say 'keeping up the caliber'? It must not only be kept up; it should be improved!

"What this industry needs most—or at least what TV news needs—is a generation of properly qualified administrators to follow the one that is passing from the scene now. And technicians and correspondents and cameramen, of course. The mechanics of TV news production are easy to teach, but the development of a 'news sense' and qualities of leadership can't be taught. We need bright men and women with good education who have cut their teeth on the hard rocks of news experience from the ground up—at a radio or TV station, or working for a newspaper or wire service. Nobody starts at the top, and nobody is born skilled or smart or dedicated. These are things you learn after a lifetime in the news business. We hope that, in the future, the best of the crop of youngsters with ambition and ability will knock on the networks' doors. We'll let them in—if they have the stuff and if they have done their apprenticeships at the local level. That's the advice I've given my own children, and you can pass it along for what it's worth."

It sounded like the real thing, coming from Bill McAndrew, President of NBC News.

Richard S. Salant, President of CBS News, does *not* look or sound grandfatherly or even fatherly. Whether his own five children think he does is beside the point. Salant looks and sounds like what he was before he went into broadcasting back in 1952: a lawyer (Harvard Law School, class of 1938). But he gives you the impression that had he stayed with his original profession, he would have been the sharpest lawyer in the entire United States!

Shirt sleeves and a lack of pretension give you a first impression of Salant, a young-looking man upon whom half a century or so of living seem to have left few permanent souvenirs. His talk is fast and direct; his answers, rapid, glib and logical almost to a fault. You get the feeling in conversation with him, as you do from many good lawyers, that nothing he says is "off the record," that he is talking to you straight from the hip and that he knows his own mind. Dick Salant's head of hair is full and brown, his smile confident and winning and his conversation engaging. In his CBS office on 57th Street in New York City, he operates five color TV screens from a panel behind his desk that looks like the control board of a spaceship. He inherited it from his predecessor.

When a visitor enters his office, all the TV monitors are shut off immediately! "I wanted to have the darn screens taken out of the office," he laughed, "but when I discovered they cost $80,000, I figured I could learn to live with them. Each shows a different network, one monitors our New York station, and one is on a feedline that carries rehearsals, preparations for shows and the intramural running of tapes — programs for the future that you're not supposed to see! So forget what you saw when you came in. That was an unfinished documentary on the loneliness of old age that we're editing now."

One of Salant's most engaging characteristics is the

skeptical look he gives you when you produce a loaded question. This was exactly how he peered at us when we asked him what he thought CBS-TV news would be like in twenty-five years.

"I'm a practical guy," he answered, "and all through my life I've tried to take one thing at a time. No matter what changes occur in broadcasting in the next generation, TV news will never—and I mean *never*—make the kind of money for a network like CBS that the entertainment shows make. All I can think of is the immediate challenge—that is, getting more network time on CBS for news programs. That's first! And, of course, it's imperative to upgrade that news—to improve it in every way possible; and that, of course, means a lot of things.

"Here at CBS, the operation is quite different from NBC. CBS news is *not* responsible for the news broadcasts of its owned and operated stations or for any of its affiliates. NBC is, in various ways. One thing we on the network level have to learn to do is to stop duplicating—or stop our stations from duplicating—the kind of news coverage the network can do and does best. This may sound simple, but it's a difficult problem. Each of us—local stations and network—should put most steam behind what it does best."

Salant adjusted his brown tortoise-shell eyeglasses and graciously held a lighter to his visitor's cigarette. "My job is essentially to expand and improve network news shows here at CBS. I don't want to get into any long discussions as to why they should or shouldn't be expanded. I'm pretty clear on most of the arguments on all sides! Suffice it to say that it's up to me to look after the welfare of the CBS network news operation; and a job is a job. What I have specifically in mind is a ten-year plan—no, by gosh, it's a *nine*-year plan now—to reach that objective. There's nothing revolutionary about it, and I may not be sitting in this chair by the time it's realized, but it's a realistic plan for *this* network — considering our economic position and the realities of news broadcasting. No pie in the sky.

"Let's remember that the revenue from TV broadcasting comes from advertisers — right? So the bulk of TV programming around the clock is not going to be news — nor would it serve any purpose if it were. Advertisers will buy time on news shows, but not the same way they pay for entertainment. Also, as far as news broadcasting is concerned, forget what you've heard about Toll-TV and other off-beat schemes. People aren't going to pay for what they get now free."

Salant took complete control of the discussion like the anchor man on a bobsled. "News broadcasting represents about one-fifth of our present service on CBS. Personally, I might prefer four-fifths, but to achieve that the news operation would have to be self-supporting, and that will never happen as long as advertising is at the financial base of this industry! And that it will be for a long time to come."

We brought up the possibilities of commercial advertisers deserting the TV industry entirely. "C'mon," said Salant with a smile, "don't talk like a Madison Avenue executive. Nothing or nobody is going to change what works! My objective — the nine-year plan — is to broaden the base of news coverage by the CBS network so that newscasts will find their way to the general audience, the women viewers who watch TV during the day and the young audience — children — who are virtually ignored by network news broadcasters at present. I want to see our news programs go directly to them!"

"The way this plan should end up," continued Salant, "is the following package on a weekly basis — all provided by the CBS *network*, remember, and *in addition to* the news that the local stations broadcast. We (the network) should provide one daily hour of hard news — no feature stuff or fun and games — after 6:30 or 7:00 in the evening. Also, the network should run — in prime time and weekly, at least — a one-half-hour hard news show centered directly on the main story of the week. Coverage in depth, if possible. Also, along with this, we should program at least one half hour of network news, designed for the housewife, that is broadcast between 10:00 A.M. and 5:00 P.M. every weekday. On Saturdays, a full half hour of news for children should be scheduled. And a full-hour documentary, feature or 'magazine' broadcast should be — will be — presented weekly in the prime evening hours at a regular time. I'm talking about *objectives* now!"

Salant continued, "In sum total, then, what have we done? We've increased the *amount* of network news CBS offers its stations. We've expanded the kind of coverage that will be given the news *every* week, and not just occasionally, as in the case of documentaries. And we've expanded the possibilities of reaching a far wider and significant audience than at present. There's nothing revolutionary about this concept. At certain times, you might even say we run such a service already. What I have in mind will regularize the CBS news operation without rearranging the network so drastically that it will cave in, which couldn't be done anyway. These formats will nevertheless put CBS way out in front of the 'competition,' in both depth and breadth of news coverage — that is, if they are well conceived and produced."

Salant was talking sense, and he knew it. We asked him what was wrong with CBS news coverage at present, and he retorted. "Wrong? Plenty's wrong, and it's exactly what some people consider right. Take our coverage of wars

— in Israel or Vietnam or anywhere. I ask you, how can TV cover a war? It can bring little bits and pieces of it, usually more dramatic than accurate, into your living room in full color! Do you want that? Do you need it? No — at least, I don't. What you *do* need is sensitive, intelligent and interesting correspondents who can *interpret* the *meaning* of warfare to you in terms that you can understand clearly. That was Ed Murrow's talent, wasn't it — to interpret, to communicate? Neither you nor I want a lot of guerrilla skirmishes in our homes, I hope! What we want is sense. At least, that's what we want from our newscasters.

"That's point one. Second, until the equipment we use is miniaturized — and I hate to blame any of our problems on gadgets — we are at the mercy of the tyranny of technology. Nothing, but nothing, ever happens the same way it was after you put a TV or movie camera on it! The fundamental problem is that TV reporters are so conspicuous that, without intending to, they can't help but influence their own coverage. And after we develop a camera and sound system that is almost invisible, we'll probably have to worry about invading people's privacy! We'll never be in the clear! As we solve one problem, another pops up."

The lawyer in Salant came to the surface as he told us that he, personally, would never permit television trials in court — but would make exceptions for the Supreme Court, "where issues, not human beings are on trial. People need to understand issues."

"You'd be surprised," laughed Dick Salant, "at the amount of independence this particular division of CBS has. So long as we don't interfere too much with network operations, we can expand, we can explore, we can search out new dimensions." A faraway look came over Salant's face. "But new dimensions cost money, and the risks and frustrations in this industry are enormous, and it's growing more expensive and complicated every day."

Salant suddenly shot up in his seat. "Now don't ask me if I regret leaving the law business for broadcasting! The answer is 'NO' and you can spell that with a capital 'N'!"

Elmer W. Lower looks just slightly out of place in the large office suite of the President of ABC News, as out of place as the giant TV console (with three picture tubes) that stands lifeless against one wall looking as if it has not been used much or frequently. Lower's corpulent frame is attired in a well-fitting conservative black suit, his black shoes are shined, his knit maroon tie reflects good taste, his thin black hair is neatly combed back, and his white shirt bespeaks custom-made perfection.

Yet something is wrong, and it takes the perceptive visitor a few minutes to figure out precisely what. Then the revelation comes in an instant to an inveterate moviegoer or TV fan: Elmer Lower belongs behind the littered desk of a managing editor of a newspaper—a crusading newspaper of the kind they write plays and movies about—talking into an old-fashioned two-piece telephone, discussing the present political situation with a city hall boss and calling him by his first name!

Until 1953, life had type-cast Elmer Lower into this role—that is, both *Life* with a capital "L," for which he was a foreign correspondent for six years, and the other "life," which kept Lower hard at work until 1953 as a print journalist. With enough newspaper background to fill this page, Lower entered the radio-TV world in 1953 and has since worked in key positions for all three networks. He has been President of ABC News (replacing ex-President Eisenhower's Press Secretary, James C. Hagerty) since 1963.

After nearly fifteen years in the world of network TV, a kidney-shaped, modernistic desk still does not seem to belong with Elmer Lower! Talk to him for ten minutes and his chair has swiveled back, his feet are crossed, shoe soles upwards, on the desk, and he is conversing with you as if he has known you all his life, or yours. Like many newspapermen, he is relaxed and intimate, even when tricky questions are being fired at him. His lack of pretension reminds one more of the school of hard knocks than Lower's true academic background, which consists of an undergraduate degree from the University of Missouri and an M.A. from Columbia University.

"I guess I was just waiting for someone to ask me about the future of TV news," he said in reply to our opening question. "Just yesterday I drafted a statement for nobody in particular about what I thought TV news would be like in twenty years. Want to see it? I have a copy around somewhere."

We said we did, and a secretary emerged with a typed onionskin carbon of a single sheet of paper. It was untitled. Here it is:

> Television news, in 1988, will be greatly expanded in quantity, vastly improved in quality, and the speed of coverage will be almost instantaneous. It will penetrate to almost all corners of the earth, even to remote African and Latin American villages.
>
> In the U.S. there will be a nightly news magazine of the air which will include instant documentaries of varying lengths on topical subjects, developed the day a story breaks. News on the hour will be as common on network television as it is today on network radio.
>
> The increased number of synchronous communication satellites will bring the far corners of the earth closer to the United States, and, conversely, will deliver world news to every country with the same-day speed.

The miniaturization of both film cameras and electronic cameras will make them so light and unobtrusive that much of the television news coverage will have the touch of far-improved *cinema verité*.

Satellite coverage will be supplemented by film delivered to the United States by supersonic planes that will cross the Atlantic in two hours and the Pacific in five.

"Of course," Lower added when we had finished reading, "a statement like this is based entirely upon assumptions that are true right *now*. Who knows how things may change? Certainly not me! I think it's entirely possible, for instance, that public demand for entertainment-type TV will diminish so much in twenty years that a major network like ABC *might* be offering an alternate nonfiction TV service made up *entirely* of news and sports, say. With the opening up of the Ultra-High-Frequency band, there will be far more TV channels available than there are at present, and why shouldn't different kinds of TV attract different — and new — viewers? This is a possibility worth thinking about."

Lower laughed. "Evidence exists that people are getting bored with the kind of entertainment TV we're giving them these days. Only one of the programs in the 'top twenty' this season is a new show. The rest are the old reliables. Yet one of the biggest single events in the season so far was ABC's four-hour special program on *Africa*. You've got to admit that was not only a program, it was an *event*!"

We admitted that it was an event, and a remarkable one at that.

"Don't look for blockbusters like the Africa show every season! But you *may* look for more news coverage every evening and more special shows from ABC every week. The number has increased since I took this job in 1963 and will continue to increase. This is the trend, and a healthy one it is."

In his casual manner, Lower continued. "Nothing is especially *new* at the moment in TV spot coverage, except color and the growing stature of the medium. This increased prestige will create a shift in the economics of the TV industry that I think will have to result in the further development and eventual maturity of this news medium.

"Look, it's common sense. One of two outcomes of the present situation is inevitable. First, either more advertisers will have to decide (correctly, I think) that news broadcasts are good vehicles for them — and this has been the direction in which the medium has been going in the past decade — with the result that good news broadcasting will become good business. Advertisers will be less interested in the large audiences that entertainment programs attract than the quality audience, the specific viewer profile, of the five, six or seven million viewers of our news programs. That's one possibility.

"Another is that the over-all profits of the TV industry will rise so enormously that more and more TV news will be underwritten by the networks every week, even if they continue to lose money. This is an unbelievably profitable business! True, all of the networks have suffered financial setbacks, but these were (and are) internal financial problems. ABC's news operation has multiplied financially, from a little over three million, ten times in the late 1950s to a $33-million-a-year enterprise right now! When you have an industry expanding at this rate, with this profit potential, you won't hear many squawks about losing a relatively few dollars on a respectable and well-run news service, especially if the viewers want it. And they *do*, whether or not advertisers are interested in news programs."

Lower's feet were on the floor now, and he was talking to us as if *we* were deciding the fate of TV news. A keen note of conviction edged his still casual, conversational tone. "I'm personally willing to settle for more and better news broadcasting, even if ABC doesn't take the lead in the industry, simply because we'll be forced to follow or compete. I'm delighted at the growth of educational broadcasting and public broadcasting, or whatever you want to call it. I wouldn't even object to an American BBC, a quasi-governmental TV system. All of these concepts promise one thing to me: more competition in this business — competition for viewers. Competition *will* drive us to do what we do better, to be more inventive and to meet wider public needs!

"Why, for instance, do the three networks always need to imitate one another by offering, as some of our critics correctly observe, more or less exactly the same kind of daily coverage of the same news stories? We don't have to, and the possibilities for differential coverage of news by the three networks are fascinating. What's going on now is not competition; it's just 'keeping up.' If we were really competing, the three networks would be using every trick in this game to be as different, one from the other, as possible."

"Which brings me to another point," Lower continued. "There is talk about increasing audiences by sensationalizing news coverage: putting more emphasis on violence and crime, for instance. I don't think that would work, simply because the viewers would never stand for it. We are a *national* medium, and the family audience will no more stand for bad manners from us than they would from national magazines. It wouldn't be respectable, and TV news coverage, at least, must keep up its traditions of respecta-bility.

"Now, I *don't* mean that there is no room for more *popular* news in place of some of the ponderous and heavy coverage on the networks today. I don't mean sensational-ism. If our operation moved in that direction, I'd resign tomorrow. I'm talking about news stories about people instead of complex issues and coverage of stories concern-ing matters that affect the viewers' daily lives. Nor do TV news programs have to be dull. We devote much time and effort here to what we call 'back of the show' items — that is, news features carefully and specially prepared in advance on some subject, trivial or important, geared to popular interest and cleverly and interestingly written and produced."

Elmer Lower again swung his feet onto the desk. "I think the future looks pretty darn exciting, and I think I'm a very lucky guy to have the job of keeping ABC News pointed in the right direction. I get my pleasure these days from the accomplishment of others, mostly the poeple on the ABC News staff. The best, I think, is yet to come. Let's see!"

Epilogue

What a long trip! From the Civil War photographs of
Mathew Brady to the early growing pains of TV news, to
the Rose Garden of the White House, to the riot-littered
streets of Newark, New Jersey, to London and Paris, to
the fancy offices of network moguls.

We have expressed our appreciation to seventy people in
the introduction to this volume for their help in writing it.
We did *not* thank the taxi driver in Washington who gave
us his own version of the capital's political picture.
No mention was made of the kind receptionist at the CBS
"cow barn" who straightened out our twisted appointment
schedule. Nor did we thank the anonymous lady reporter
who told us the juicy "inside story" of the social life
among White House correspondents.

The people we got to know *best* are in the pages you
have just read. Almost without exception they were intelligent, helpful and talented people, so much so that we
would like to take one more full-length look at them before
we close our typewriter cover and call it a day.

Both authors have, in the course of their careers met, interviewed, eaten with, worked with and even lived with a vast number of individuals who work (and sometimes play) in the fascinating world of mass communications. We know publishers, writers, actors, artists and all sorts of craftsmen who labor in countless corners of the book, newspaper, television, radio and motion picture industries, doing all manner of jobs. We also number among our acquaintances men and women in the advertising business, press agents and innumerable teachers and professors of what are presently called "the communication arts." And we have worked closely with numerous idea invaders who try to carry messages of freedom and democracy across national boundaries to totalitarian societies overseas by print and radio.

We consider many of these individuals fine people personally and professionally, and we are proud that they call us by our first names and even — occasionally — share their experiences and troubles with us, officially and unofficially.

We were, however, due for a surprise when we ventured into the TV news offices of the networks and various local stations. We do not mean to denigrate in any manner the colleagues of these TV newsmen who work in other media or to raise our noses to the artists involved in the entertainment side of the TV industry. Far from it. But our impression of the sincerity, dedication and skill of the men and women behind the cameras (and in front of them) in the TV news business came to us as an unexpected and delightful surprise.

Almost without exception, the people who bring the news to us on TV have two major objectives that they seem to pursue with every means at their command. First, they have their jobs to do in attempting, with neither bias nor favor, to make good an obligation we know they feel: to present to the American public as much of the news as they can, as clearly, swiftly and fairly as possible. This objective is understood so universally in the TV newsrooms we visited that we rarely heard it spoken. It was taken for granted, and the newsmen we interviewed imagined that we took it for granted too. We did not when we started writing this book. We do now.

Second, the other great objective of all TV newsmen on all levels — and we are aware of how sweeping this generalization sounds — is to do their jobs so well that the viewing public will demand of their employers more hours of news coverage per day, more completely presented and told in greater detail than at present.

If our TV newsmen are, by and large, aware of one major shortcoming in their efforts, it is the assumption, unfortunately and frequently mouthed by print journalists, that TV cannot cover the news of the day in depth and from different points of view the way the print media do. The broadcasters know that this bit of "folk wisdom" is simply untrue, and, in the light of the experiences that produced this book, we agree with them without reservation.

TV can be the most powerful news medium the world has yet known, to quote one of our enthusiastic broadcasters. It *can* tell the details of news stories with breadth and scope that would rival the skills of the finest newspaper writers. It *is able* to articulate clearly as many points of view as a stack of editorials in print, with clarity and verve that would rival the arts of Horace Greeley or James Gordon Bennett. TV has the potential for covering as wide a spectrum of human interest as a Sunday magazine section, a picture magazine, or a weekly journal of news and opinion. Its scope is nearly unlimited.

TV can do all of these things. Not only is the medium

capable of it, but so are the people who are working in it today: the men and women you see on your TV screen at home and the countless others you do not see who work beside them but never appear "on camera." All of them are deeply involved in their various jobs right now. But we are certain that they are ready and able to increase their efforts to the degree that their respective employers might decide to increase both the time and the scope of their TV news operations. In our travels, we have heard this promise time and time again, from errand boys on motorcycles to executives in offices in skyscrapers. And we are trusting enough to believe that most of these people meant what they said, because the intensity of their conviction was unmistakable and the potential of their abilities was obvious.

We also sensed from these people a keen edge of dissatisfaction, of incompleteness and frustration in their work, merely because their best efforts were so infrequently called forth, and because they were afforded so few opportunities to demonstrate the fullness of their talents. When a president of the United States meets a Soviet leader, the TV news people are given a chance to stand at full height. When a race riot ravishes a city, or when a world crisis shocks the national nerve, they can demonstrate the power of the TV medium and their own potentials as newsmen and women. But only then.

Day after day, however, they are asked, usually, to inhabit the fringes of the TV schedule, to tell their stories as quickly and as painlessly as possible and then to move on to make way for antique motion pictures or TV "personalities" whose tired jokes and creeping unpopularity are forever blamed on a fickle public. The public, of course, is not fickle; it is remarkably loyal to individuals of talent and stature, be they entertainers like Jack Benny or newsmen like the late Ed Murrow.

We are not crusaders, and a plea for quality on our TV screens is as absurd as a plea for virtue — on the side of the angels, but of little relevance to practical matters in the broadcasting industry.

If the American public, however, makes known its demands for wider and more extensive news coverage, it must receive it, for the reason that nearly every public in every democracy gets the kind of TV service it wants — or deserves. In the United States, the men who manage our TV stations know that giving the people what they want is good business. If the people make known their desires and needs for more and fuller TV news coverage, the network and station managers will have to satisfy them, like it or not.

The destiny of TV news, in other words, is up to *us*. What are we going to do about it? The people who are ready to cover the action want to know!

Suggested Reading

Suggested Readings

Anonymous, *There Was a President*. New York: Ridge Press Inc., 1966.

Barnouw, Eric, *A Tower in Babel*. New York: Oxford University Press, 1966.

Bluem, A. William, *Documentary in American Television*. New York: Hastings House, 1965.

Bluem, A. William, and Manvell, Roger, editors, *Television: The Creative Experience*. New York: Hastings House, 1967.

Buxton, Frank, and Owen, Bill, *Radio's Golden Age*. New York: Easton Valley Press, 1966.

CBS News, *Television News Reporting*. New York: McGraw-Hill, 1958.

Ceram, C. W., *Archeology of the Cinema*. New York: Harcourt, Brace and World, 1965.

Dary, David, *Radio News Handbook*. Thurmont, Maryland: Tab Books, 1967.

Dizard, Wilson P., *Television, A World View*. Syracuse, New York: Syracuse University Press, 1966.

Emery, Edwin, Ault, Philip H., and Agee, Warren K., *Introduction to Mass Communications.* New York: Dodd, Mead, 1960.

Emery, Edwin, and Smith, Henry L., *The Press and America.* New York: Prentice-Hall, 1954.

Friendly, Fred W., *Due to Circumstances Beyond Our Control.* New York: Random House, 1967.

Grauer, Ben, editor, *NBC News Picture Book of the Year 1967.* New York: Crown, 1967.

Harmon, Jim, *The Great Radio Heroes.* New York: Doubleday, 1967.

Head, Sidney W., *Broadcasting in America.* Boston: Houghton Mifflin, 1956.

Knight, Arthur, *The Liveliest Art.* New York: The New American Library, 1959.

Mayo, John B., Jr., *The President Is Dead.* New York: Exposition Press, 1967.

Montagu, Ivor, *Film World.* Baltimore: Penguin Books, 1964.

Mosse, Baskett, and Whiting, Fred, editors, *Television News Handbook.* Evanston, Illinois: Medill School of Journalism, Northwestern University, 1953.

Murrow, Edward R., *In Search of Light, The Broadcasts of Edward R. Murrow 1938–1961.* New York: Knopf, 1967.

Murrow, Edward R., and Friendly, Fred W., *See It Now.* New York: Simon and Schuster, 1955.

National Council of Teachers of English, *TV as Art.* Champaign, Illinois, 1966.

Paulu, Burton, *Radio and Television Broadcasting on the European Continent.* Minneapolis: University of Minnesota Press, 1967.

Settel, Irving, *A Pictorial History of Radio.* New York: The Citadel Press, 1960.

Shulman, Arthur, and Youngman, Roger, *How Sweet It Was.* New York: Shorecrest, 1966.

Siller, Bob, White, Ted, and Terkel, Hal, *Television and Radio News.* New York: Macmillan, 1960.

Skornia, Harry J., *Television and Society.* New York: McGraw-Hill, 1965.

Swallow, Norman, *Factual Television.* New York: Hastings House, 1966.

Wood, William A., *Electronic Journalism.* New York: Columbia University Press, 1967.

Index

Index

About The Authors

GEORGE N. GORDON is presently a professor and director of the Communications Center at Hofstra University in Hempstead, New York. A graduate of the Yale Drama School, he received his Ph.D. degree from New York University, and is now a broadcaster, teacher and author. He hosted his own radio program, *The Lively Arts*, for WCBS, was an associate professor of Communications in Education at New York University, and has written or co-authored eight non-fiction books. He has also found time to travel extensively in North Africa and Europe and lecture and consult frequently on the psychology and social roles of mass communications. Dr. and Mrs. Gordon and their three children live in New York City.

IRVING A. FALK is presently Associate Professor in the Film and Television Institute of the School of the Arts at New York University. He attended Washington Square College, the Yale Drama School and Columbia University and has been a broadcaster, teacher, author, producer-director, information editor and actor. He has written, editor and co-authored six books. The series, *By The Year 2000*, which he produced with his students at New York University, has been syndicated nationally and abroad. For eight years he has produced *The Urban League Presents* and he has been Assistant to the Executive Officer of the Communication Arts Group at New York University. He lives in Fair Lawn, New Jersey, near the place of his birth in Paterson.